A Short Guide to
the Pronunciation of
New Testament Greek

**EERDMANS
LANGUAGE
RESOURCES**

The Eerdmans Language Resources series is
a collection of textbooks, readers, reference
books, and monographs pertaining to
languages commonly used in biblical and
theological studies. In these volumes,
students and scholars will find indispensable
help in understanding and mastering Hebrew,
Aramaic, Greek, and other languages.

Other ELR Titles

A Short Guide to the Pronunciation of New Testament Greek

Benjamin Kantor

WILLIAM B. EERDMANS PUBLISHING COMPANY

GRAND RAPIDS, MICHIGAN

Wm. B. Eerdmans Publishing Co.

4035 Park East Court SE, Grand Rapids, Michigan 49546

www.eerdmans.com

Published 2023

Printed in the United States of America

29 28 27 26 25 24 23   2 3 4 5 6 7

ISBN 978-0-8028-7832-8

Library of Congress Cataloging-in-Publication Data

A catalog record for this book is available from the Library of Congress.

Τω Υιω μου Τω αγαπητω εν ω Ευδοκησα

Contents

Symbols and Abbreviations

#	indicates word boundary in IPA notation
_	placeholder for sound in question: e.g., _b = when sound occurs before [b]
//	in English text, encloses phonemic transcription
[ ]	in English text, encloses phonetic transcription
[ ]	in a Greek text, encloses restoration of fragment or missing text
( )	in a Greek text, encloses completion of abbreviation or suspension
AOR	aorist
BCE	before common era
c.	century
C	consonant: e.g., CV
CE	common era
CLSP	Cross Language Speech Perception
CSG	common singular
FSG	feminine singular
FUT	future
IMPV	imperative
IND	indicative
IPA	International Phonetic Alphabet
NOM	nominative
NPL	neuter plural
PN	personal name
PNTG	Benjamin Kantor, *The Pronunciation of New Testament Greek: Judeo-*

Palestinian Greek Phonology and Orthography from Alexander to Islam.
Grand Rapids: Eerdmans, 2023

PRES	present
SLA	secondary language acquisition
SUBJ	subjunctive
V	vowel: e.g., CV

So You Want to *Read* (Pronounce) Biblical Greek

I t is only a matter of time before the student of Biblical Greek faces a series of somewhat controversial questions regarding the "correct" or "appropriate" pronunciation of the language: How was Biblical Greek pronounced? How do we know how Biblical Greek was pronounced? How *should* Biblical Greek be pronounced? The controversial nature of such questions, however, does not necessarily lie in the ambiguity of the evidence, but rather in the history of the field of Biblical Greek pedagogy.

Though the most common pronunciation of Biblical Greek taught in seminaries across the world today bears the name of Desiderius Erasmus (i.e., the "Erasmian" pronunciation), it was probably not used by Erasmus himself. In fact, the evidence would suggest that Erasmus learned to speak a contemporary form of Greek (i.e., "modern" Greek of the fifteenth century), and thus, when he read the New Testament, he read it with a pronunciation similar to that heard in Greece today (see 1.4). The pronunciation named after him was merely a speculative reconstruction based on Erasmus's work regarding how ancient Greek must have been pronounced in light of the best available evidence at the time.

Many who use an "Erasmian" pronunciation to teach Biblical Greek today do so merely out of convention, knowing full well that the historical pronunciation was otherwise. Indeed, one need read only a handful of papyri from the Koine period before being faced with a series of spelling interchanges that simply cannot be explained from the perspective of a Classical, Traditional, or "Erasmian" pronunciation. Still others, notwithstanding the excellent work that has been done by a number of scholars on the pronunciation of Greek during the Koine period,[1] claim that we really cannot know exactly how Koine Greek was pronounced. For this group, there is no reason to abandon the convention, though not strictly historical, if it would not be replaced by something well-established and certain.

The scientific and pedagogical purpose of the present volume—along with its larger companion volume (see below)—is to engage both of these groups in a scholarly conversation by establishing the pronunciation of Judeo-Palestinian Koine Greek[2] at the time of the New Testament (and comparing it with other contemporary regional varieties of the Koine) and presenting the findings in an engaging and welcoming manner accessible even for beginning students of Biblical and Koine Greek. The present volume is actually a practical digest version of the much larger and more academically rigorous volume *The Pronunciation of New Testament Greek: Judeo-Palestinian Greek Phonology and Orthography from Alexander to Islam* (henceforth *PNTG*).[3] *PNTG* constitutes a comprehensive analysis of the spelling conventions attested in roughly 4,500 Judeo-Palestinian inscriptions and papyri from the Hellenistic period through to the end of Byzantine times. These data are then used to reconstruct the pronunciation of Judeo-Palestinian Greek and chart its development throughout these periods. This smaller digest volume constitutes a pedagogically minded summary of the findings of *PNTG*. Its purpose is twofold: (i) to provide a concise "how to" guide for the historical pronunciation of New Testament Greek (based on Judeo-Palestinian Greek of the Roman period); and (ii) to make the case that using a historical pronunciation of Koine Greek is pedagogically best for students learning the language.

---

1. See chapters 1 and 6 in *PNTG*.

2. Note that "Judeo-" in the term "Judeo-Palestinian" is regional (i.e., province Iudaea) and not religious or ethnic (Jewish).

3. *The Pronunciation of New Testament Greek: Judeo-Palestinian Greek Phonology and Orthography from Alexander to Islam* (Grand Rapids: Eerdmans, 2023).

This volume begins with a history of Greek pronunciation in pedagogy (chapter 1), which treats the impact of Erasmus's fable on the pronunciation of Greek used in the classroom since the Renaissance period. This is followed by a brief outline of the methodology of historical Koine Greek phonology, that is, how we know how Koine Greek was pronounced (chapter 2), and a short excursus on some basic concepts in phonetics and phonology that will help the reader better appreciate the rest of the book (chapter 3). This is followed by a concise pronunciation guide for Koine Greek of the Roman period with a particular emphasis on Judeo-Palestinian Greek (chapter 4). The final chapter treats some of the pedagogical issues regarding Koine Greek pronunciation as it relates to Second Language Acquisition (SLA) and other considerations (chapter 5). The book concludes with a selection of sample practice texts in International Phonetic Alphabet (IPA) transcription. A select subject bibliography on historical Greek phonology, Koine dialectology, historical linguistics, the history of pronunciation in pedagogy, and applied SLA/pedagogy is found at the back of the book.

1

How Has Greek Been Pronounced in the Classroom since Erasmus?

1.1 INTRODUCTION

As demonstrated by ancient conversational handbooks from the Greco-Roman world,[1] people have been formally learning Greek in a school setting for millennia. Pronunciation never seems to have been a contentious issue, however, up until the modern era. Before then, it seems that Greek was learned in the contemporary pronunciation of native Greek speakers. To put it simply, until about the fifteenth century, Greek had always been taught in a "modern" Greek pronunciation, that is, in the native pronunciation of contemporary Greek speakers.[2] What follows is a brief historical overview of how this general trend began to change beginning in Renaissance times.

---

1. Eleanor Dickey, *Colloquia Monacensia–Einsidlensia, Leidense–Stephani, and Stephani* , vol. 1 of *The Colloquia of the Hermeneumata Pseudodositheana* (Cambridge: Cambridge University Press, 2012); Eleanor Dickey, *Colloquium Harleianum, Colloquium Montepessulanum, Colloquium Celtis, and Fragments* , vol. 2 of *The Colloquia of the Hermeneumata Pseudodositheana* (Cambridge: Cambridge University Press, 2015).

2. Presumably, however, the specific pronunciation in any given context would have been subject to conscious and subconscious modifications according to the vernacular and orthography of the region. There were also likely situations in which the "school" pronunciation was slightly more conservative than the "colloquial" pronunciation (see *PNTG* §8.3.2.1.I).

1.2 THE EARLY RENAISSANCE PERIOD

Already by the thirteenth and fourteenth centuries, it seems that knowledge of Greek had essentially dried up in Latin-dominant Western Europe.[3] The English philosopher Roger Bacon (1214–1292) is famous for saying in 1267 that "there were not five men in Latin Christendom acquainted with Greek grammar." The Italian scholar and poet Petrarch (1304–1374) noted a century later that Italy could boast of no more than eight or nine Italians who knew Greek.[4] During the Renaissance period, Greek could be learned either from native Greeks (in Greece or abroad) or from the humanist scholars who had learned Greek from a non-Greek source.[5] The beginning of the modern era of Greek learning in Europe really did not begin until 1397, when Manuel Chrysoloras was appointed as Professor of Greek in Florence.[6] It was not until the fall of Constantinople in 1453, however, that a significant wave of Byzantine scholars moved west to Italy and intensified the revival of Greek learning in Europe, taking their knowledge and pronunciation of Greek with them.[7]

As the study of Greek began to experience a revival in Europe, students and scholars alike soon realized that the native "modern" pronunciation of Greek, that is, the Byzantine one, did not always coincide with the pronunciation reflected in the ancient texts being studied.[8] This is

3. But note Petrounias's comments on Calabria in southern Italy, where a number of Greek monasteries maintained a presence. Naturally, they used a "modern" or Byzantine pronunciation of Greek there. See E. B. Petrounias, "The Pronunciation of Ancient Greek in Modern Times," in *A History of Ancient Greek: From the Beginnings to Late Antiquity*, ed. A.-F. Christidis (Cambridge: Cambridge University Press, 2007), 1266.

4. James Morwood, *The Oxford Grammar of Classical Greek* (New York: Oxford University Press, 2001), 7.

5. Janika Päll, "Far Away from Byzantium: Pronunciation and Orthography of Greek in the 17th Century Estonia," in *Byzantino-Nordica 2004: Papers Presented at the International Symposium of Byzantine Studies Held on 7–11 May 2004 in Tartu, Estonia*, ed. Ivo Volt and Janika Päll (Tartu: Tartu Univeresity Press, 2005), 87–88.

6. Eugenia Russell, "Book Review Essay: Greek in the Renaissance: Scholarship, Dissemination and Transition," *Renaissance Studies* 25, no. 4 (2011): 585.

7. Morwood, *Classical Greek*, 7.

8. Karl Feyerabend, *Handy Dictionary of the Greek and English Languages* (New York: David McKay Company, 1918), vi.

most apparent in the pronunciation of the vowels indicated by ι, η, υ, ει, οι, and υι, which were all pronounced with the same sound: IPA [i].[9] In fact, this problem had already been recognized by Byzantine Greek scholars such as Maximos Planoudes of Constantinople, who noted that the following words were all pronounced in the same way: ἐρήμην 'by default', ἐροίμην 'I would ask', αἱρεῖ μιν 'he will seize him', αἱροίμην 'I would choose', ἐρεῖ μιν 'he will say it', αἱροίμην 'I would lift', ἐρρίμμην 'I had been thrown'.[10] The "modern" or Byzantine pronunciation of Greek, which hardly would have differed from the pronunciation of Modern Greek today, soon came to be regarded as inadequate. The Byzantine Greeks, who were regarded as the great teachers of Western scholars when they first migrated, thus came to be held in lower esteem.[11] What followed was a number of attempts by various scholars to reconstruct the more "original" or "correct" pronunciation of ancient Greek.[12]

1.3 ERASMUS'S GENERATION

The first of these was Antonio of Lebrixa (Antonio de Nebrija) (1444–1522), a Spanish humanist who, in 1503, argued that η was a long vowel corresponding with ε, that ω was a long vowel corresponding with ο, and that ζ was pronounced as σδ. He eventually outlined an entire system for the pronunciation of the Greek letters and suggested altering the pronunciation of ancient Greek. Aldus Manutius (1449/1452–1515), a Venetian scholar, soon contributed his own insights, famously noting that the bleating sound of sheep, βῆ βῆ, was not pronounced as [vi vi] but as [bɛː bɛː]. He is also famous for establishing the *Neacademia*, an academy for philologists, the members of which had to communicate in ancient Greek. This same group would eventually host Erasmus himself in 1508. The Italian cardinal Girolamo Aleandro (1480–1542), who intro-

---

9. IPA stands for the International Phonetic Alphabet, which is a universal standard notation system for transcribing sounds of a language. For background on the IPA and its use in this volume, see §3.2.

10. Petrounias, "Ancient Greek in Modern Times," 1267.

11. R. A. McNeal, "Hellenist and Erasmian," *Glotta* 53, no. 1/2 (1975): 83.

12. Morwood, *Classical Greek*, 7.

duced Greek teaching to the University of Paris, was also one of the early
scholars to weigh in on this debate. It should be noted, however, that all
these early scholars' forays into the field of historical Greek phonology
were mostly theoretical, pointing out supposed disparities between the
"modern" Byzantine pronunciation and the ancient pronunciation.[13]

1.4 Erasmus and His Fable

Although the work of Antonio of Lebrixa, Aldus Manutius, and Girolamo Aleandro served as cracks in the dam of the Byzantine "modern"
pronunciation of Greek, it was Desiderius Erasmus (1466–1536), a Dutch
Christian scholar and humanist, who opened the floodgates. In 1528, in
the guise of an amusing conversation between a bear and a lion, Erasmus
penned his famous *De recta Latini Graecique sermonis pronuntiatione*
('Concerning the right pronunciation of Latin and Greek speech'), in
which he both criticized the contemporary "modern" pronunciation of
Greek and outlined *the foundation* of what has come to be known today as the "Erasmian" pronunciation of Greek. Though it was originally
thought that this treatise was mistakenly inspired by a joke, this opinion
has since been refuted.[14] It is more likely that Erasmus's ideas came from
his discussions with the Byzantines during his time in Venice.[15] Erasmus's dialogue was likely a sincere academic exercise, but speculative
enough not to be taken too seriously due to its light-hearted presentation. Its intention seems to have been more about reflecting an academic
conversation going on at the time rather than about making a definitive
argument about the proper reconstruction of the language.[16] Erasmus's

13. Ingram Bywater, *The Erasmian Pronunciation of Greek and Its Precursors: Jerome
Aleander, Aldus Manutius, Antonio of Lebrixa: A Lecture* (Oxford: Oxford University Press,
1908); McNeal, "Erasmian," 88–89; Morwood, *Classical Greek*, 7; Petrounias, "Ancient
Greek in Modern Times," 1268; Russell, "Review of Greek in the Renaissance," 585–86.

14. For the most recent articulation of this view, see Chrys C. Caragounis, "The
Error of Erasmus and Un-Greek Pronunciations of Greek," *Filología Neotestamentaria*
8 (1995): 151–85. For the refutation of the view, see Jody A. Barnard, "The 'Erasmian'
Pronunciation of Greek: Whose Error Is It?," *Erasmus Studies 37* (2017): 109–32.

15. Petrounias, "Ancient Greek in Modern Times," 1269.

16. Barnard, "Erasmian," 114.

motivation for jettisoning the Byzantine pronunciation and developing a new reconstructed pronunciation seems to have been undergirded by three principles: (i) that the past was radically cut off from the present, (ii) that ancient writers should be able to speak for themselves in their own voice, and (iii) that the Greek alphabet came into being to accurately correspond to and reflect the sounds of the language.[17]

The work begins with Lion, who having just fathered a newborn cub, asks Bear for advice about how to find a first-class grammarian to tutor his cub. Bear's response is that of a good classicist, lauding the priority of Greek and Latin and firmly encouraging adherence to the correct pronunciation, reading, and writing of these languages. Though the dialogue covers many different issues, central to its flow is the affirmation that the majority or "modern" pronunciation of Greek in use at the time was incorrect. Greek had undergone phonological change since the ancient period and thus had incurred a significant degree of "corruption." Having sufficiently demonstrated the inadequacy of the contemporary pronunciation, Bear goes on to outline the original pronunciation of ancient Greek by proceeding through the correct reconstruction of the entire alphabet, all the while making frequent appeals to other (non-Greek) European languages to buttress his case. [18]

The reconstruction offered by Bear is a bit idiosyncratic, not necessarily aligning with any modern version of "Erasmian" pronunciation. Barnard has reconstructed the pronunciation suggested by Bear in Erasmus's dialogue as follows.[19]

TABLE 1.4-1: RECONSTRUCTION OF "ERASMIAN" VOWELS AND DIPHTHONGS

α = [a]	αι = [a] + [i]	αυ = [a] + [y]	
ε = [ε] η = [e]	ει = [ε] + [i]	ευ = [ε] + [y]	ηυ = [e] or [y]
o = [ɔ] ω = [oʊ]	οι = [o] + [i]	ου = [o] + [y] or [aʊ]	
υ = [y]	υι = [y] or [i]		
ι = [i]			

17. McNeal, "Erasmian," 86–87.
18. Barnard, "Erasmian," 114–21.
19. Barnard, "Erasmian," 114–21.

TABLE 1.4-2: RECONSTRUCTION OF "ERASMIAN" CONSONANTS

VOICELESS UNASPIRATED STOPS:	π = [p]	τ = [t]	x = [k]
VOICED UNASPIRATED STOPS:	β = [b]	δ = [d]	γ = [g]/[ŋ]
VOICELESS ASPIRATED STOPS:	φ = [fh]	θ = [θ]	χ = [χ]
FRICATIVES:	σ = [s]	' = [h]	
LIQUID RESONANTS:	λ = [l]	ρ = [r]	
NASAL RESONANTS:	μ = [m]	ν = [n]	
COMBINATIONS:	ζ = [sd]	ψ = [ps]	ξ = [ks]

Of particular note are the diphthongal realization of ω [oʊ]; the front high rounded realization of the υ element [y] in the diphthongs αυ, ευ, ου, and ηυ; the fricative yet aspirated realization of φ ([fh]); and the affricate realization of ζ as [sd]; none of which accord with modern "Erasmian" pronunciations.

Before proceeding any further, however, it is necessary to stop here and address the question of Erasmus's own practice in reading Greek himself. Though he is credited with establishing the reconstructed pronunciation of ancient Greek used throughout universities and schools across the world today, the evidence suggests that Erasmus both learned and continued to read Greek according to the "modern" native pronunciation of his time and *not* the reconstructed pronunciation. This is most clearly evidenced by his *Familiar Colloquies*, in which he rhymes the following Greek words with Latin words ending in *i* (IPA [i]): ὄνοις, κόποι, λάροι, λόγοι, εἰκῇ, and λύκοι. The fact that Erasmus maintained these "rhymes" in later iterations of the work, even after the publication of *De recta Latini Graecique sermonis pronuntiatione*, suggests that he continued to pronounce ancient Greek with a "modern" pronunciation throughout his life.[20]

Thus, any so-called modern "Erasmian" pronunciation follows neither Erasmus's practice nor his original reconstruction in the mouth of Bear. We require one more stage in the history of Greek pedagogy to

---

20. McNeal, "Erasmian," 87–88; Matthew Dillon, "The Erasmian Pronunciation of Ancient Greek: A New Perspective," *Classical World* 94, no. 4 (2001): 324–25, 334; Barnard, "Erasmian," 113–15.

arrive at the precursors of what today are termed "Erasmian" pronunciations. Following the publication of Erasmus's widely circulated and read treatise, what had before been an academic curiosity among a select number of scholars had now become a hot academic debate. Indeed, it may be more appropriate to refer to Erasmus as a "popularizer" rather than as an innovative scholar on this point. This debate led to further modifications of Erasmus's theory, parallel scholarly reconstructions not directly derived from Erasmus, and the practical application of these "reformed" pronunciations in various institutions. There were, however, those who resisted the new reconstructed pronunciation. Johannes Reuchlin (1455–1522) is perhaps the most famous example of a scholar from this era who resisted the efforts to reconstruct a new pronunciation and maintained the Byzantine pronunciation as this debate was beginning to swell.[21] For this reason, the traditionalist school of thought in this debate has often been termed either the "Byzantine" or "Reuchlinian" school.[22] This would set the stage for how this debate would play out and its ultimate ramifications for Greek pedagogy in the coming centuries.

1.5 THE AFTERMATH OF ERASMUS'S FABLE

In the years immediately following the publication of Erasmus's treatise, the positions of various institutions regarding pronunciation largely broke down according to denominational lines. The Byzantine pronunciation found continued use among the Lutheran, Catholic, and Jesuit schools, whereas the reconstructed "Erasmian" pronunciation seems to have been mainly a possession of the Calvinists. It was not until the end of the sixteenth century that the reconstructed pronunciation gained greater acceptance among a wider range of churches.[23]

21. Russell, "Review of Greek in the Renaissance," 585.
22. Päll, "Greek in the 17th Century Estonia," 86–87.
23. Engelbert Drerup, *Die Schulaussprache des Griechischen von der Renaissance bis zur Gegenwart, im Rahmen einer allgemeinen Geschichte des griechischen Unterrichts. Erster Teil: Von XV bis zum Ende des XVII Jahrhunderts* (Paderborn: Schöningh, 1930), 220–22, 278–408; Päll, "Greek in the 17th Century Estonia," 86–87.

In England, credit for the implementation of the "reformed" pronunciation goes to two Cambridge scholars, John Cheke and Thomas Smith. Soon after their election as Regius Professors of Greek and Civil Law in 1540, they began to implement their version of the reconstructed pronunciation, which was not actually based on Erasmus's pronunciation. Actually, their reconstruction was probably a closer and more accurate, though by no means perfect, reflection of what Classical Attic pronunciation is now thought to have been. Their efforts soon met with pushback, however, when the Chancellor of the University, Stephen Gardiner, forbade the use of this new pronunciation in the university in 1542.[24] It was not until 1558 that this rule was finally repealed.

One special characteristic of the pronunciation of Greek that would develop in England concerns the accent system. Following Isaac Vossius (1618–1689) and Heinrich Christian Henning (1635–1684), who argued that the standard accents were not original and that ancient Greek accent patterns must follow those of Latin, English Greek came to be accented according to a Latin pattern.[25] In Latin stress rules, the antepenultima is normally stressed unless the penultima is a heavy syllable, in which case the penultima is stressed: e.g., *princípium*, but cf. *salvéte, amátis*, and *firmáméntum*. Therefore, a Greek word like ἑλληνική would be stressed on the syllable -λη- rather than -κή and a Greek word like ἄνθρωπος would be stressed on the middle syllable -θρω- instead of the first syllable ἄν-. Even to this day one can still find those in England who have been taught Greek according to this pattern, though it has largely faded out of use.

Though England initially led the charge in embracing the new "ancient" pronunciation, the Great English Vowel Shift (GVS) of the sixteenth century complicated matters.[26] Previously, scholars could

24. For a more in-depth look at the academic and political conflict between Stephen Gardiner and John Cheke, see John F. McDiarmid, "Recovering Republican Eloquence: John Cheke versus Stephen Gardiner on the Pronunciation of Greek," *History of European Ideas* 38, no. 3 (2012): 338–51.

25. Alain Ballabriga, "Philhellénisme et prononciation du Grec. À propos de la 'Dissertation sur la prononciation grecque' de Fleury de Lécluse," *Anabases* 3 (2006): 69.

26. The Great English Vowel Shift consists of the raising and/or diphthongization of long vowels, as in the following words: /i:/ → /aɪ/ (e.g., [biːt] → [baɪt] = bite); /e:/,

coordinate the reconstruction of the ancient Greek vowels with their corresponding English vowels. After the shift, the Greek vocalic system required a reconfiguration as it related to English. A set of reforms was eventually introduced by the end of the nineteenth century that helped realign the official pronunciation with that of ancient Greek. This was followed by a series of publications by Cambridge University Press further refining the reconstruction of the ancient pronunciation, the most famous of which—and still of value today—being Allen's *Vox Graeca*.[27] These more recent publications and reforms have largely corrected many of the earlier errors in English Greek pedagogy.

It should be noted, however, that even at a relatively late stage along the way, there were also voices that tried to call English Greek pedagogy back to the Byzantine or "modern" pronunciation, such as E. M. Geldart (*The Modern Greek Language in Its Relation to Ancient Greek*)[28] and John Stuart Blackie, Oxford professor of Classics (*The Pronunciation of Greek*).[29] Ultimately, however, such appeals were unsuccessful.

In France, after an "Erasmian"-type pronunciation was adopted, it came to be reshaped over the coming centuries in accordance with the

---

/ɛː/ → /iː/ (e.g., [meːt], [mɛːt] → [miːt] = meet, meat); /aː/ → /eɪ/ (e.g., [maːt] → [meɪt] = mate); /uː/ → /aʊ/ (e.g., [huːs] → [haʊs] = house); /oː/ → /uː/ (e.g., [boːt] → [buːt] = boot); /ɔː/ → /oʊ/ (e.g., [bɔːt] → [boʊt] = boat). See Lyle Campbell, *Historical Linguistics: An Introduction* (Cambridge: MIT Press, 1999), 48.

27. Morwood, *Classical Greek*, 8. For works at the end of the nineteenth century and during the twentieth century documenting and refining the reconstruction of the pronunciation of ancient Greek in the wake of these reforms, see E. V. Arnold and R. S. Conway, *The Restored Pronunciation of Greek and Latin* (Cambridge: Cambridge University Press, 1895); James Morwood, *The Teaching of Classics* (Cambridge: Cambridge University Press, 2003); and, of course, the famous W. Sidney Allen, *Vox Graeca: A Guide to the Pronunciation of Classical Greek* (Cambridge: Cambridge University Press, 1968).

28. E. M. Geldart, *The Modern Greek Language in Its Relation to Ancient Greek* (Oxford: Clarendon, 1870), 1–40. Geldart advanced the opinion that "the same phonetic laws were at work in the time of Homer and of Thucydides as are at work now, and they produced the same results" (40). Although this is a misguided exaggeration, his work demonstrates considerable insight. If he had merely advanced his dating several centuries to the Hellenistic or Koine period, he would not have been far off.

29. See John Stuart Blackie, *The Pronunciation of Greek; Accent and Quantity: A Philological Inquiry* (Edinburgh/London: Sutherland and Knox/Simpkin, Marshall & Co., 1852).

characteristics of French. According to Ballabriga, this led to the French pronunciation of Greek being especially divergent from "Erasmian" in comparison with the Italian or Spanish pronunciation of Greek. Nevertheless, there were still those who opposed the new reconstructed pronunciation, such that it never became universal in France. The "anti-Erasmian" group, which seems to have arisen in the seventeenth century, included scholars such as Adamantios Korais (Ἀδαμάντιος Κοραῆς) (1748–1833). Korais was a Greek scholar living in France at the time, who suggested that the modern pronunciation had its beginnings in the Hellenistic period and was to be preferred over "Erasmian."[30] This sentiment was continued by notable linguistic work of nineteenth-century French scholars, such as Fleury de Lécluse (1774–1845), Gustave d'Eichthal (1804–1886), and Émile Egger (1813–1885). This wave of scholars attempted to reform pedagogical practice in France with respect to the pronunciation of ancient Greek. A conference was even held in 1896 to examine the possible benefits that a study of the pronunciation of Modern Greek could yield. Their attempts, however, were met with little enthusiasm. The wave of *Philhellénisme* of the nineteenth century never quite overtook those committed to the "Erasmian" pronunciation, but its impact was not unnoticed and it remains in pockets of French academia to this day.[31]

Italy, like France, never lost its strong connection with Greece and thus witnessed its own wave of *Filellenismo* in the eighteenth and nineteenth centuries. By this time, the "Erasmian" pronunciation had become more universal and dominant in educational institutions. Nevertheless, the scholars of the *Filellenismo* movement, who were regarded as supporters of the "Eastern" system, fought to revive the "modern" or Byzantine pronunciation for teaching ancient Greek. Much like their counterparts in France, however, they were largely unsuccessful.[32] An Italian version of the "Erasmian" pronunciation remains the primary pronunciation of ancient Greek in Italy to this day.

In Germany, the new "Erasmian" pronunciation was initially resisted by the Lutheran Protestants, who preferred to maintain the traditional

30. Petrounias, "Ancient Greek in Modern Times," 1270.
31. Ballabriga, "Philhellénisme."
32. Petrounias, "Ancient Greek in Modern Times," 1270.

"modern" or Byzantine pronunciation. One reason for the reluctance of the Lutheran churches to accept Erasmus's reconstruction must have been the heated theological dispute that took place between Eramsus and Luther during the Reformation. Luther also had as a close companion one of the staunchest defenders of the Byzantine pronunciation in Johannes Reuchlin. As the "Erasmian" pronunciation eventually took hold, adherents of Erasmian came to be known as *Etazisten* ('etacists') and the adherents of the Byzantine pronunciation came to be known as *Iotazisten* ('iotacists'), in accordance with their pronunciation of the letter η as /e/ or /i/, respectively.[33]

In the Baltic region, there seem to have been several different schools and methods for teaching Greek at a relatively early period. The *Academia Gustaviana*, as part of the second most prestigious university in the Swedish Empire, recommended using only the Byzantine or "modern" Greek pronunciation, as evidenced by the Greek Grammars of Clenardus (1495–1542) and Gualtperius (1543–1624). In both grammars, "modern" Greek values were assigned for each of the Greek letters with no separate treatment of the diphthongs. In subsequent grammars of the mid-seventeenth century (and in a later printing of Clenardus's grammar), both the Byzantine and the "Erasmian" realizations were included for certain key letters such as β and η. Indeed, a combination of evidence from spelling mistakes, puns in Greek texts, and transliterations of foreign words suggests that the "Erasmian" pronunciation had gained significant ground in the seventeenth century. By the end of the seventeenth century, there are records that schoolboys in the region were failing to distinguish ε from η, which suggests that they were using an "Erasmian" pronunciation. Päll concludes that the old "modern" or Byzantine pronunciation must have been replaced by the "Erasmian" pronunciation during the seventeenth century.[34]

In Greece, of course, the "modern" or Byzantine pronunciation continued to be used and remains the normal pronunciation for teaching ancient

---

33. Petrounias, "Ancient Greek in Modern Times," 1270.

34. Päll, "Greek in the 17th Century Estonia," 92–113. Note that Päll's study applies specifically to Estonia. It is likely, however, that some of the same conclusions apply to the wider region.

Greek to this day. The "Erasmian" pronunciation, on the other hand, is not looked upon with favor by educated Greeks. Though not always historically or linguistically well grounded, there is a sentiment that accepting the "Erasmian" pronunciation would constitute an "affront to national pride."[35] A more balanced approach in favor of the modern pronunciation accepts that although the pronunciation of Hellenistic Greek was remarkably close to Modern Greek, the pronunciation of Plato and Aristotle remains a good distance away from those on the streets of Athens today.

1.6 "ERASMIAN" PRONUNCIATION IN THE PRESENT DAY

The situation of the present day is the natural outgrowth from the trajectory set several centuries ago. As a reconstructed "Erasmian" pronunciation gained popularity and came to be utilized in different countries, it gradually came to mirror the orthographic and phonological characteristics of each region's vernacular. So, for example, though Erasmus reconstructed the aspirated stops as φ [fʰ], θ [θ], and χ [χ], Germans pronounce them as [f], [θ]/[tʰ], and [kʰ] in accordance with German phonology. English speakers tend to pronounce the unaspirated stops π [p], τ [t], and κ [k] with aspiration as [pʰ], [tʰ], and [kʰ], in accordance with the realization of plosives in their native phonology, even though Erasmus reconstructed them as unaspirated. The consonant ζ also exhibits a good deal of variety, being pronounced as [dz] in English and Italian, [ts] in German, and [z] in French. Variation also occurs in the pronunciation of the diphthongs, so that ευ is pronounced by English speakers as [uᵘ] (or [ju]), by German speakers as [ɔi], and by French speakers as [ø]. The multivariate nature of "Erasmian" today is nicely illustrated by the various pronunciations of the word ζεύς (Classical Greek: [dzéᵘs] or [zdéᵘs]): English [dzuᵘs] (or [dzjus]); German [tsɔis]; French [zøs]; Italian [dzeᵘs]; Modern Greek [zefs].[36] With such variation among academic communities today, one wonders how strong the argument is that the "Erasmian" pronunciation provides a scholarly standard to ease communication between scholars of disparate origins.

35. Petrounias, "Ancient Greek in Modern Times," 1271.
36. Petrounias, "Ancient Greek in Modern Times," 1273–75.

The differences between the basic sounds of a Byzantine/Modern Greek pronunciation, the reconstructed pronunciation of Erasmus's fable, and an American "Erasmian" pronunciation can be depicted in the chart below.[37]

TABLE 1.6-1: PRONUNCIATION COMPARISON:
BYZANTINE/MODERN, ERASMUS'S FABLE, AND AMERICAN "ERASMIAN"

GREEK LETTERS	BYZANTINE/MODERN	ERASMUS'S FABLE	AMERICAN "ERASMIAN"
α	[ɑ]	same	same
β	[v]	[b]	[b]
γ	[ɣ], [j]	[g]	[g]
γ(γκξχ)	[ŋ]	[ŋ]	[ŋ]
δ	[ð]	[d]	[d]
ε	[ẹ]	[ɛ]	[ɛ]
ζ	[z]	[sd]	[ds] or [dz]
η	[i]	[e]	[e] or [eɪ]
θ	[θ]	same	same
ι	[i]	same	same
κ	[k]	same	same or [kʰ]
λ	[l]	same	same
μ	[m]	same	same
ν	[n]	same	same
ξ	[ks]	same	same
ο	[ǫ]	[ɔ]	[ɔ]
π	[p]	same	same or [pʰ]
ρ	[r]	same	[ɹ]
σ ς	[s̩], [z]	[s], [z]	[s], [z]
τ	[t]	same	same or [tʰ]
υ	[i]	[y]	[u]
φ	[f]	[fh]	[f]
χ	[x], [ç]	[χ]	[χ]
ψ	[ps]	[ps]	[ps]
ω	[ǫ]	[oʊ]	[oʊ]

37. The chart is taken and adapted from Barnard, "Erasmian," 120–21.

DIGRAPHS/DIPHTHONGS

GREEK LETTERS	BYZANTINE/MODERN	ERASMUS'S FABLE	AMERICAN "ERASMIAN"
αι	[ẹ]	[α] + [i]	[aɪ]
αυ	[αv], [αf]	[α] + [y]	[aʊ]
ει	[i]	[ɛ] + [i]	[e] or [eɪ]
ευ	[ẹv], [ẹf]	[ɛ] + [y]	[ju]
ηυ	[iv], [if]	[e] or [y]	[ju]
οι	[i]	[o] + [i]	[ɔi]
ου	[u]	[o] + [y] or [aʊ]	[u]
υι	[i]	[y] or [i]	[wi]
BREATHINGS	Ignored	Observed	Observed
ACCENTS	Observed	Observed	Observed/Ignored

The story of the pronunciation of ancient Greek in pedagogy can be summarized in several stages. From antiquity until the beginning of the modern era, ancient Greek was normally taught with the contemporary Greek pronunciation of native speakers. Around the turn of the sixteenth century, due to a renewed interest in Greek in Europe, scholars began to experiment with reconstructing the original pronunciation of ancient Greek. Erasmus eventually popularized this debate through his famous fable, in which he speculatively reconstructed the original pronunciation of ancient Greek. This idea immediately took hold of the scholarly world, quickly leading many universities to institute reforms, either adopting the "Erasmian" pronunciation or another similar reconstruction. Though there was some pushback initially, within a century or two some form of the reconstructed pronunciation had become the norm for Greek teaching on the continent. Despite its dominance, however, there were some attempts in different countries, such as France and Italy, to move back to a "modern" or more Hellenistic pronunciation of Greek. These attempts of the so-called "Philhellenism" movement, however, were unsuccessful. As time progressed, the "Erasmian" pronunciation multiplied in form, both due to scholarly revisions of the reconstruction and due to the natural assimilation of the pronunciation to features of the orthography and phonology of local vernaculars. All the while, the traditional "Byzantine" or "modern" pronunciation, used by Erasmus himself and his predecessors, was maintained essentially only in Greece.

1.7 BACK TO BYZANTIUM:
NEOHELLENIC (MODERN) AND "LIVING KOINÉ"

More recent times have been witness to, once again, a renewed interest in using either the modern pronunciation or a sort of restored "Hellenistic" or "Koine" pronunciation, which resembles the modern pronunciation in most of its phonological features. Scholarly arguments for using a Neohellenic (i.e., modern) pronunciation in Greek pedagogy have been put forward by Cohen and Sellers, Theophilus, Lee, Campbell, and Zachariou.[38] Caragounis also advocates for a Neohellenic pronunciation by pointing out that what we now call Modern Greek pronunciation was already emerging in ancient times.[39] Dillon takes a bit more conservative approach, arguing that we should take Modern Greek as a starting point and make a number of modifications to bring it more into conformity with ancient Greek.[40] Buth is probably the most well-known advocate for a restored "Living Koiné" pronunciation, having developed it for teaching Koine Greek communicatively.[41] Accordingly, he strikes a threefold balance between the historical phonology of the Koine period, continuity with the modern language, and ease of utterance for English speakers. The "Living Koiné" pronunciation thus has all the first-century CE vowels (according to Buth), but substitutes the late-Roman/Byzantine fricatives φ [ɸ], θ [θ], χ [x], and δ [ð] for the first-century CE stops φ [pʰ], θ [tʰ], χ [kʰ], and δ [d].[42] To a native Greek, the "Living Koiné"

---

38. Gary G. Cohen and C. Norman Sellers, "The Case for Modern Pronunciation of Biblical Languages," *Grace Theological Journal* 5 (1984): 197–203; Michael P. Theophilus, "On the Pronunciation and Interpretation of 'Biblical Greek': A Re-Assessment in Light of the Papyri" (Paper presented at the University of Cambridge New Testament Seminar, 6 November, 2012); Constantine Campbell, *Advances in the Study of Greek: New Insights for Reading the New Testament* (Grand Rapids: Zondervan, 2015), 192–208; Philemon Zachariou, *Reading and Pronouncing Biblical Greek: Historical Pronunciation Versus Erasmian* (Eugene, OR: Wipf & Stock, 2020). For Lee, see Campbell, §9.3–4.

39. Caragounis, "Error of Erasmus."

40. Dillon, "Erasmian Pronunciation."

41. Randall Buth, "Ἡ Κοινὴ Προφορά: *Koiné Pronunciation;* Notes on the Pronunciation System of Koiné Greek," Biblical Language Center (2012): 1–10.

42. In some dialects, φ might already have been a fricative by the first century CE (see §4.1.5). Note also that δ probably did not come to be pronounced as [ð] until the third century CE (see §4.1.3).

pronunciation sounds essentially identical to their own system with the addition of two vowels: η = [e] and οι/υ = [y].[43] A comparison of the basic sounds of historical (first-century CE) Koine Greek phonology, Buth's "Living Koiné", and Modern Greek is depicted below.

TABLE 1.7-1: PRONUNCIATION COMPARISON: HELLENISTIC/KOINE,
BUTH'S "LIVING KOINÉ," AND MODERN GREEK

GREEK LETTERS	KOINE GREEK (ACTUAL)	BUTH'S "LIVING KOINÉ"	MODERN GREEK
α	[ɑ]	[ɑ]	[ɑ]
β	[β]	[β]	[v]
γ	[ɣ] or [j]	[ɣ] or [j]	[ɣ] or [j]
δ	[d]	[ð]	[ð]
ε	[e̞]/[ɛ]	[ɛ]	[e̞]
ζ	[z]	[z]	[z]
η	[e]	[e]	[i]
θ	[tʰ]	[θ]	[θ]
ι	[i]	[i]	[i]
κ	[k]	[k]	[k]
λ	[l]	[l]	[l]
μ	[m]	[m]	[m]
ν	[n]	[n]	[n]
ξ	[ks̲]	[ks]	[ks̲]
ο	[o̞]	[o]	[o̞]
π	[p]	[p]	[p]
ρ	[r]	[r]	[r]
σ ς	[s], [z]	[s], [z]	[s], [z]
τ	[t]	[t]	[t]
υ	[y]	[y]	[i]
φ	[pʰ]/[ɸ]	[ɸ]	[f]
χ	[kʰ]	[x]	[x]
ψ	[ps̲]	[ps]	[ps̲]
ω	[o̞]	[o]	[o̞]

43. Also note that in the Buth system the consonants β and φ (and υ in the diphthongs αυ/ευ) are pronounced historically as [β, ɸ] instead of [v, f] as in Modern Greek.

GREEK LETTERS	KOINE GREEK (ACTUAL)	BUTH'S "LIVING KOINÉ"	MODERN GREEK
DIPHTHONGS			
αι	[ẹ]/[ɛ]	[ɛ]	[ẹ]
αυ	[aβ(ʷ)], [aɸ(ʷ)]	[aβ], [aɸ]	[av], [af]
ει	[i]	[i]	[i]
ευ	[ɛβ(ʷ)], [ɛɸ(ʷ)]	[ɛβ], [ɛɸ]	[ẹv], [ẹf]
ηυ	[eβ(ʷ)], [eɸ(ʷ)]	[eβ], [eɸ]	[iv], [if]
οι	[y]	[y]	[i]
ου	[u]	[u]	[u]
υι	[yi̯] or [y]	[yi̯] or [y]?	[i]
ʽ	[h] or ø	ø	ø

All of this renewed interest in Greek pronunciation in pedagogy cul-
minated in an entire SBL session devoted to the topic in 2011, with pre-
sentations by Oliver Simkin (overview of historical Greek phonology),
Daniel Wallace (Erasmian), Randall Buth (reconstructed Koine), and Michael Theophilus (Modern Greek). Most recently, Philemon Zachariou
has published an entire monograph on the subject, entitled *Reading and
Pronouncing Biblical Greek: Historical Pronunciation versus Erasmian.* In
his book, Zachariou endeavors to show both the tremendous historical
depth that the Neohellenic pronunciation has and the problematic nature of using the Erasmian pronunciation.[44] Finally, Luke Ranieri, who
has done excellent work in developing communicative Latin and Greek
materials online, has pioneered what is called the "Lucian" pronunciation of Ancient Greek,[45] which is fairly reflective of a more formal, high,
and/or literary register of the second century CE (but with some com-
promises to bridge the gap between Classical and Modern Greek).

In my view, there have been several factors that have contributed to
this renewed interest in pronunciation and pedagogy in recent decades.

44. Zachariou, *Pronouncing Biblical Greek.*

45. See Luke Ranieri, "Ancient Greek Pronunciation Guide and Discourse on the
Inherent Challenges of Establishing a Single Ancient Greek Pronunciation System
with Detailed Explanation of the Lucian Pronunciation of Ancient Greek," published
online at LukeRanieri.com, December 2020, revised January 2021.

First, a number of works on Koine Greek phonology were published during the twentieth century, greatly increasing our knowledge of the topic. Second, over the past century the fields of Divinity (theology, biblical studies, etc.) and Classics have become separated from each other in a way that would have been foreign to scholars of Erasmus's day or even to scholars of a century ago. This has led to great swaths of seminary students (and professors) only ever studying Koine Greek, and often only a very restricted corpus within the category of Koine Greek, namely the New Testament and/or the Septuagint. Interestingly, such a narrow focus among a large portion of those involved in Greek studies has actually freed advocates of pronunciation reform from answering objections that would apply only to Classical Greek. Third, advances in the field of Second Language Acquisition (SLA) have demonstrated the need for fluent production when learning a foreign language. Naturally, this has led to a renewed focus on questions of pronunciation (see more in §5.3).

Fourth, and finally, the establishment of the modern state of Israel and the revival of the Hebrew language has revealed the benefits of fluency for biblical language study. Because Modern Greek is assumed—perhaps incorrectly—to be more different from Koine Greek than Modern Hebrew is from Biblical Hebrew, the benefits of learning Modern Greek have not been as obvious to ancient Greek scholars. Because of the high degree of overlap between Modern Hebrew and Biblical Hebrew, however, the advantages are more difficult to ignore.[46] This, in turn, has raised the question whether the same might not be done for Biblical Greek. Consequently, there has been an increased focus on the balance between practicality and historical authenticity in the pronunciation one uses to learn ancient Greek.

---

46. There are several reasons why Modern Hebrew has received more attention among Biblical Hebrew scholars than Modern Greek has among Ancient Greek scholars. First, the pronunciation of Modern Hebrew is one of the main accepted pronunciations of Biblical Hebrew today. Second, the morphology of Modern Hebrew is in many respects identical with that of Biblical Hebrew, albeit with certain exceptions. Finally, regrettably, there also seems to be a deep-seated divide between Greece and the rest of Europe in the history of Greek scholarship since the Renaissance. See Zachariou, *Pronouncing Biblical Greek*, 75–115.

1.8 REFLECTIONS

It is against such a backdrop, at the end of a long line of succession, that the current volume on the pronunciation of Koine Greek in Judea-Palestine steps onto the stage. Throughout the modern era, the pronunciation of Greek in pedagogy has always been inextricably linked to advances in the study of historical phonology. Though Erasmus's original reconstruction is inaccurate in many ways, it was originally composed as a scientific inquiry and not a pedagogical one. It is curious, then, that most of its advocates today favor it for pedagogical reasons rather than scientific ones. After all, Erasmus continued to use the Byzantine or "modern" pronunciation himself, even after the publication of his treatise. Moreover, as more advances were made in the field of historical Greek phonology, scholars modified the reconstructed pronunciation further.

Indeed, one wonders if the scholars of Erasmus's generation would have felt the need to jettison the Byzantine pronunciation had they known what we now know about the pronunciation of Koine Greek. In fact, some have suggested that the departure from the "modern" or Byzantine pronunciation in Erasmus's day was as much political and ideological as it was academic. The need to abandon the "modern" Greek pronunciation in favor of a reconstructed "ancient" pronunciation seems to have been at least partly predicated on the idea that the purity of the distant past had been corrupted by the ignorance of the "dark ages." The inability to accept the linguistic continuity between the ancients and the moderns, which had never been a problem for the Greeks, seems to have been one of the primary issues underlying the motivation of Western scholars to develop a new pronunciation tradition of their own. One might add to this the simple yet humbling truth that, since the fall of Constantinople, modern Greece has largely been off the radar for many Western scholars of ancient Greek.

Therefore, the idea that "majority use" or "convention" are sufficient enough reasons to perpetuate the status quo when we now know much more than our predecessors did about the continuity between Koine Greek and Modern Greek is neither academically defensible nor historical. Especially today, when so many students of Greek know it only in its Koine attire, there is no reason not to allow advances in our understanding of Koine Greek phonology to also impact our pedagogy.

Though not all of the authors of the New Testament were Judeo-Palestinian Jews, the inextricable connection between "The Land" and the Greek New Testament is self-evident. Accordingly, what is now needed to advance the field, both academically and pedagogically, is a new work devoted specifically to the pronunciation of Koine Greek in Judea-Palestine. Indeed, reflecting on the past thirty years of Greek linguistic study as it relates to pronunciation, Porter writes the following:

> Even if there are more advocates for types of historic or modern pronunciation than there were earlier, we may have developed in the depth of our knowledge, but there is little [new] that we know now that was not known before. There is much more said, to be sure, but not much development.[47]

Porter is not wrong in his assessment. It has now been more than forty years since the last comprehensive treatment of Koine Greek pronunciation. And such studies have mostly been confined to Egypt.[48] While forming a complete picture of the various dialects, sociolects, idiolects, etc. of Koine Greek at the time of the New Testament will not be complete until similar studies have been carried out for the Greek of Italy, Asia Minor, and other locales in the Mediterranean, this current project (i.e., *PNTG* and this companion digest volume) can at least close the gap with respect to the Judeo-Palestinian material. Hopefully, it can help close the gap in reforming (or at least informing) our pedagogy as well.

---

47. Stanley E. Porter, "So What Have We Learned in the Last Thirty Years of Greek Linguistic Study?," in *Getting into the Text: New Testament Essays in Honor of David Alan Black*, ed. Daniel L. Akin and Thomas W. Hudgins (Eugene, OR: Pickwick, 2017), 17.

48. But cf. §1.2–3 in *PNTG*. Note also that Slavova's recent work (2004) on the phonology of Greek inscriptions in the Bulgaria region (ancient Thrace)—as covered in §1.3 of *PNTG*—is fairly comprehensive. Mirena Slavova, *Phonology of the Greek Inscriptions in Bulgaria* (Stuttgart: Franz Steiner Verlag, 2004).

2

How Do We Know How Koine Greek Was Pronounced?

2.1 Spelling "Mistakes"

A continuous echo of skepticism resounds around the field of historical Koine Greek phonology, not often from those working on the material themselves, but rather from those merely passing through the corridors. That is to say, despite the well-researched and well-established developments posited for the pronunciation of Greek during the Koine period (see chapters 1 and 6 in *PNTG*), there are nevertheless those who regard such reconstructions as chasing after smoke. It is my contention that, though we do have to be careful not to overinterpret the data, there is actually considerably more evidence for certain developments in the pronunciation of Koine Greek than for certain contemporaneous historical events!

With such divergent attitudes toward the material, the importance of a clear and robust methodology is paramount. As simple as it may seem, the primary method for reconstructing the pronunciation of ancient Greek consists of tabulating and analyzing the spelling "mistakes"—more neutrally referred to as interchanges or variation—of a given corpus. This process may be best illustrated with a series of examples in English. Take, for example, the English word *tough*. If someone misspelled it as *tuff*, another person analyzing the text might conclude that *ou* was equivalent to *u* in this context, both being pronounced as

IPA [ʌ], and that *gh* was equivalent to *ff* in this context, both being pronounced as IPA [f]. Similarly, if the English word *perceive* was misspelled as *percieve*, another individual analyzing the text might conclude that *ei* was equivalent to *ie* in this context, both being pronounced as IPA [i]. Finally, we might take a slightly more complex example. Imagine analyzing a document with a series of misspellings of the word *read*, sometimes rendered as *reed* and sometimes as *red* At first glance, one might suggest that this means that *ea*, *ee*, and *e* were all equivalent in this context and were pronounced as IPA [i]. Imagine that upon closer examination, however, it becomes clear that misspellings with *ee* are used only in a present-tense context and misspellings with *e* are used only in a past-tense context. In light of such a distribution, one could then claim only that *ea* was equivalent to *ee* in present-tense instances of the word *read*, both being pronounced as IPA [i], whereas *ea* was equivalent to *e* in past-tense instances of the word *read*, both being pronounced as IPA [ɛ]. Such an example demonstrates how easy it can be to misinterpret the data if one is not careful to consider other factors such as morphology and syntax.

Having demonstrated how the process works through English examples, let us now return to Greek. Take, for example the word κεῖται 'lies; is found', which is especially common in funerary inscriptions. Note, for example, the standard phrase found on many graves and ossuaries: ἐνθάδε κεῖται PN 'here lies PN'. At a very early stage in Classical Greek, this word was pronounced as [ˈkeːtai̯] (with pitch accent as [keétai̯]). So how do we know how it was pronounced in the Koine period? Once again, we can examine scores of funerary inscriptions for spelling mistakes. What we find is that sometimes it is misspelled as κιται, which indicates that ει was equivalent to ι in this context, both being pronounced as IPA [i]. In other cases, it is misspelled as κιτε, which indicates that αι was equivalent to ε in this context, both being pronounced as [ɛ] (or perhaps [e̞]). From these clues, we can conclude that the word was pronounced as [ˈkitɛ]/[ˈcitɛ] (note additional palatalization of initial [k] → [c]).

What, then, do we as scholars do to arrive at a reconstruction of the entire language? First, we examine the relevant corpora of papyri and inscriptions and tabulate all the spelling "mistakes"—or interchanges—contained therein, and organize them according to time and place. Then, we interpret the data, determining the implication of each spelling inter-change for pronunciation. From all of this information, we can determine when and where certain changes in pronunciation occurred. While this is a bit of an oversimplification of the process, it is a clear and succinct summary of the main principles of the method. A more detailed and rigorous outline of the methodology, as it specifically relates to this study of Judeo-Palestinian Koine Greek, is outlined in chapter 2 of *PNTG*.

2.2 GREEK LOANWORDS IN HEBREW AND ARAMAIC

Alongside a comprehensive documentation of ancient spelling "mis-takes" (i.e., interchanges), the rendering of Greek loanwords in other languages and scripts can also shed light on how Greek was pronounced historically. In our particular case, the rendering of certain Greek loan-words in Hebrew and Aramaic can help us reconstruct the pronuncia-tion of Judeo-Palestinian Koine Greek. For example, if Greek σ is ren-dered by Hebrew *samek* ס (/s/) normally but by Hebrew *zayin* ז (/z/) before a voiced consonant (e.g., προσβολή → פְּרוֹזְבּוֹל [prozvol]), this shows that Greek σ in Judeo-Palestinian Greek was probably pronounced similarly to [s] normally but as [z] when immediately preceding a voiced consonant.

The linguistic subdiscipline that studies how speakers of one lan-guage perceive and assimilate sounds from a foreign (or second) lan-guage to sounds in their native language is called Cross Language Speech Perception (CLSP). Although we must be careful in our application of a modern theoretical framework to ancient material, CLSP may serve as a helpful tool in analyzing the rendering of Greek loanwords in Hebrew and Aramaic. For a fuller discussion of CLSP as it relates to our method-ology, see §2.4 in *PNTG*.

3

Do I Need to Be a Linguist?

3.1 INTRODUCTION

One of the most difficult parts of getting into a new field is learning the terminology, conventions, and format through which ideas are communicated. It is no different with respect to the field of historical Koine Greek phonology. Accordingly, it is the intention of this short chapter to provide a brief introduction to three of the more foundational linguistic tools and/or principles used in the field: (i) the International Phonetic Alphabet (IPA), (ii) the difference between phonetics (and the phone) and phonology (and the phoneme), and (iii) the concept of language change. Although the reader can get by without knowing the IPA or the basics of phonetics/phonology, taking the time to digest these tools and principles will prove invaluable when dealing with topics of historical pronunciation and help the reader to be conversant in the wider field of historical Koine Greek phonology.

3.2 THE INTERNATIONAL PHONETIC ALPHABET (IPA)

It is near impossible to read any modern linguistic study on pronunciation or phonology without understanding the International Phonetic Alphabet. The IPA is a universally standard scientific alphabet which, theoretically, has a character for every sound of the world's languages. For many decades of philological research, each individual language discipline tended to use its own conventional system of notation for representing the actual pronunciation of words under discussion. Although the IPA was developed at the turn of the twentieth century, it took more than a century for most language disciplines to adopt it over their previous (often idiosyncratic) conventions. There are to this day, however, still some language disciplines that maintain their own traditional conventions.

In the linguistic subfields of phonology and phonetics (see below in §3.3 for the difference between the two), the pronunciation of consonants and vowels are described in two distinct ways.

Consonant sounds are described in terms of *place of articulation* and *manner of articulation*. Place of articulation refers to the point where an obstruction (with the tongue) is made to create the sound (e.g., back of the throat, top of the throat, on the lips, between the teeth). Manner of articulation refers to what the "speech organs" do when the sound is made (e.g., continuous hum, stop the sound, trill). The simplest of these to illustrate is the quality of voice (i.e., whether the vocal cords vibrate when pronouncing a consonant). For example, the only difference between the initial consonant in the word *dock* and *tock* is that the vocal cords vibrate when pronouncing the *d* but not when pronouncing the *t*. Because there are far more potential articulatory combinations for consonants than for vowels, it may take some time to become fluent in describing consonant sounds with IPA lingo. Nevertheless, a standard consonant chart including the consonants discussed in this work (related to Greek) is depicted below. The horizontal axis denotes place of articulation and the vertical axis manner of articulation. When two consonants have the same place and manner of articulation, the unvoiced consonant is on the left and the voiced consonant is on the right.

TABLE 3.2-1: SELECTION OF IPA CONSONANTS IN CHART

	BILABIAL	LABIO-DENTAL	(INTER)-DENTAL	ALVEOLAR¹	PALATAL	VELAR	GLOTTAL
PLOSIVE	p, pʰ	b		t, tʰ d	c, cʰ ɟ	k, kʰ g	
NASAL	m	ɱ		n	ɲ	ŋ	

1. Note that alveolar consonants might also have been alveodental in certain dialects of Koine Greek.

	BILABIAL	LABIO-DENTAL	(INTER-)DENTAL	ALVEOLAR	PALATAL	VELAR	GLOTTAL
FRICATIVE	ɸ β	f v	θ ð	z s	ç j	x ɣ	ʔ h
TRILL				ɽ r			
APPROXIMANT					j	w	
LATERAL				l	ʎ		

So, for example, the sound represented by the letter *b* in the word *bed* is called a voiced bilabial stop, since when pronouncing the sound, the vocal cords vibrate (i.e. voiced), both lips come together to create the obstruction (i.e., bilabial), and the sound does not continue (i.e., stop). The symbol : can be added to a consonant sign to indicate that it is long, namely, that it is held for almost or around twice the length of a regular consonant (e.g., b:).[2] It is also common, however, to represent such consonants merely by repeating the letter (e.g., bb). In either case, a consonant with such an extended duration can also be referred to as a "geminated" or "doubled" consonant. One final note that should be mentioned is the meaning of the superscript letter [h] in the symbols p[h], t[h], k[h], c[h]. The addition of a superscript [h] to an IPA symbol means that it was pronounced with following aspiration. Aspiration simply means that a noticeable puff of air comes out of the mouth as the consonant is pronounced. Specific examples of distinctions between consonants with and without this feature in English are cited in §3.3.

Vowels are described in terms of the position of the tongue in the mouth when the vowel is pronounced.[3] Depicted using the trapezium below, the horizontal axis measures vowel backness (i.e., how far for-

---

2. It is not unusual, however, for a "long" or geminated consonant to be pronounced for as little as 1.2x the regular consonant.

3. Phoneticians have described vowels in terms of "height" and "backness" for a long time, but these terms actually correspond more to acoustic frequencies than to the position of the tongue. The high-low distinction corresponds to what is referred to as the first formant (F_1) and the front-back distinction roughly corresponds to the difference between the first formant (F_1) and the second formant (F_2). See Peter

ward or how far back the tongue is in the mouth) and the vertical axis measures vowel height (i.e., how high or low the tongue is in the mouth). Height can also be measured in terms of openness of the mouth, which seems to be more common in recent literature. In addition to backness and height/openness, it is also possible to describe a vowel in terms of whether or not the lips are rounded in its articulation. Such a difference may be illustrated by the pair *tuck* and *talk*. Although the tongue is in the exact same place when pronouncing the vowels represented by *u* and *a* in these words, the vowel in *tuck* is without rounding (IPA ʌ), whereas the vowel in *talk* is with rounding (IPA ɔ). In the IPA vowel trapezium, these distinctions are shown by placing two vowel signs on the same spot, with the unrounded vowel on the left and the rounded vowel on the right. A standard vowel trapezium including the primary vowels discussed in this work is depicted below.

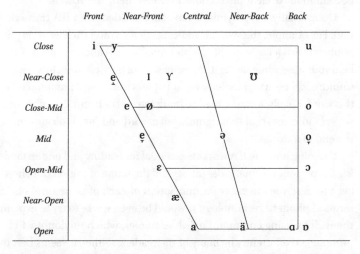

So, for example, the IPA symbol ɛ, which corresponds to the sound of the *e* in the pronunciation of the words *bed, set,* and *get,* is called a mid-low front vowel (or a mid-open front vowel), since the tongue is in a low (but not all the way) position at the front of the mouth. Finally, it

Ladefoged, *A Course in Phonetics* (Fort Worth: Harcourt College Publishers, 2001), 14–15, 170–78, 232–33.

should also be noted that the symbol : can also be added to any of these vowel signs to indicate that it is long, namely, that it is held for almost or around twice the length of a regular vowel.

At this point, I should also mention that there is another important category of sounds known as diphthongs. The word *diphthong* (from Greek δίφθογγος) literally means "with two sounds" and refers to a sequence of two consecutive vowels pronounced together in one gliding sound such as /a/ + /i/ = /ai̯/ or /a/ + /u/ = /au̯/ (the reason why IPA sounds are sometimes enclosed in / / or [ ] will be covered below in §3.3. Sometimes, diphthongs can be clearly indicated by using a superscript version of the second letter or an inverted breve below the second letter: e.g., /aⁱ/ and /aᵘ/ or /ai̯/ and /au̯/. Because diphthongs play an important role in the history of Greek phonology and they behave a bit differently than just regular vowels (e.g., in terms of their syllabification), it is important to make clear distinctions between them and vowels.

Occasionally, other symbols can also be added to an IPA transcription. For example, the symbol ˜ indicates that a vowel such as [a] is pronounced with a nasal quality (represented as [ã]) and sounds as if you held your nose while saying it. Parentheses can be used to enclose a weak sound: e.g., [ˈpe̜(n)de̜] indicates that [n] was not always pronounced in this word. Finally, # can be used to mark the end or beginning of a word, so /#r/ indicates /r/ at the beginning of a word and /n#/ indicates /n/ at the end of a word.

Grasping how the IPA works is essential for reading and understanding the present volume. It lies far beyond the scope of this section, however, to describe the exact pronunciation of each of these symbols in terms of phonetic terminology. It would be even worse to try to explain them all by using common English examples, which no doubt will be pronounced differently by many of the readers. Rather, it seems best to recommend to the reader at this point—if the concepts of the IPA and general phonetics are still somewhat shaky—to make use of the many online audio resources for learning the IPA sounds and to read the chapter on phonetics in an introductory linguistics book.[4]

4. See, e.g., Ladefoged, *Course in Phonetics.*

3.3 PHONOLOGY AND PHONETICS:
THE PHONEME AND THE ALLOPHONE

Although benefitting from this book does not depend on having a deep understanding of linguistic theory as it relates to phonology and phonetics, there is one important principle that must be firmly grasped in order to avoid confusion. This principle would actually be better termed *a distinction*, between **phonology** and **phonetics**, on one hand, and between the **phoneme** and the **allophone**, on the other.

To put it simply, there are two ways of thinking about sounds in a language. First, we may think of sounds in the way that a sound recorder processes sounds. It records the frequencies of the sound waves and converts them into real objective measurements. In this sense, there is not really any difference in quality between the sounds someone makes when they stub their toe on a toy car and the sounds someone makes when they utter, "Who left this car here?!" Both are equally products of the human speech organs. On the other hand, we may think of sounds in the way that the user of a language processes them. In this sense, there is all the world of difference between a shriek of pain and the statement, "Who left this car here?!" Only the latter prompts the listener to recognize sound patterns, words, and grammar.

In linguistic terminology, the distinction between these two ideas (i.e., the objective "sound-recorder-like" measurement vs. sounds that carry actual meaning) is described as the distinction between **phonetics** and **phonology**. Phonetics is *the study of the sounds of a language apart from any meaningful contrast*. It focuses on the physical aspects of the sounds of a language. **Phonology**, on the other hand, is *the study of the system of meaningful contrasts in the sounds of a language*. Within these two fields, we may speak of the *units* of **phones** and **phonemes**. A **phone** (phonetic unit) is *the smallest unit of sound in a language apart from any relation to meaning*. In linguistic notation and transcription, phones are typically represented between square brackets: e.g., [foʊn]. A **phoneme** (phonological unit) is *the smallest unit of sound in a language that accomplishes a difference in meaning*. In linguistic notation and transcription, phonemes are typically represented between forward slashes: e.g., /foʊnim/.

We may illustrate the difference between these two concepts through a couple of examples in English: The English word 'pool' may be represented **phonemically** as /pul/. It has two consonantal phonemes (/p/ and /l/) and one vocalic phoneme (/u/). We know that each of these sounds indicates a meaningful opposition and thus constitutes a phoneme by comparing it to other words where just one of these three sounds is swapped out: e.g., 'fool' /ful/, 'cool' /kul/, 'pal' /pæl/, 'poof' /puf/. In each case, the change of just one sound accomplishes a difference in meaning.

On the other hand, note how the pronunciation of the consonant /p/ in the word 'happy' (/hæpi/) is different from that of the consonant /p/ in the word 'pool'. To do this, place your hand directly in front of your mouth as you pronounce each of these words. What you will find is that you feel a puff of air on your hand when you say 'pool', but not much air at all when you say 'happy'. This is because, even though the same **phoneme** /p/ is used in each instance, they are pronounced slightly different in the context based on their vocalic environment. In the word 'happy', the /p/ is pronounced without aspiration (i.e., the puff of air), and thus would be represented **phonetically** as [p]. In the word 'pool', on the other hand, the /p/ is pronounced with aspiration (i.e., the puff of air), and thus would be represented **phonetically** as [p] with a following superscript [ʰ] to indicate the aspiration: i.e., [pʰ].

Most native English speakers, unless they are linguists, have never even noticed this difference. That is because there is no place in the language where a distinction between [p] and [pʰ] accomplishes any meaningful difference. In other words, a speaker could theoretically substitute [p] for [pʰ] or vice versa in any English word and still be understood just fine. That is because [p] and [pʰ] are both **allophones** (different phones; i.e., individual sounds not accomplishing a contrast in meaning) of /p/. The same is not the case, however, for the consonants /p/ and /f/ (as shown above).

We can assume that most speakers of Koine Greek were the same, generally not noticing the difference between various phonetic realizations (i.e., **allophones**) of the same **phoneme**. Because of this lack of awareness of **allophones**, certain changes in small details of pronunciation (i.e., **phonetic** features) are unlikely to be consistently reflected in the orthography until they rise to the level of **phonemic** significance. Therefore, the distinction between **phones, phonemes,** and **allophones** is an immensely important one to grasp when analyzing our material. Because the general topic of "pronunciation" overlaps with both **phonology** and **phonetics,** but not perfectly with either of them, it will be necessary to make careful distinctions between **phonemic** and **phonetic** features throughout our analysis.

3.4 HISTORICAL LINGUISTICS

Although this pronunciation guide is focused on the pronunciation of Greek at the time of the New Testament, namely in the first century CE, it deals with material as early as the fourth century BCE and as late as the sixth and seventh centuries CE. This is because one cannot properly understand what was going on in Greek at the time of the New Testament without mapping out the trajectory of certain changes in the language both before and after the period. Therefore, it is important to give some advance attention to the linguistic discipline of historical linguistics before proceeding with the rest of the book. **Historical linguistics is primarily concerned with the topic of language change,** namely *how* and *why* languages change. In fact, historical linguistics is sometimes referred to as *diachronic linguistics* (from Greek διά 'through' + χρόνος 'time') since it deals with language change over time. This is to be contrasted with *synchronic linguistics* (from Greek σύν 'with' + χρόνος 'time'), which deals with a language at one particular point in time as a cohesive and complete entity, whether one specific stage of the language in history or the contemporary form of the language in the present day.[5] Diachronic and synchronic approches are not in conflict with one another but are actually both necessary and work together to provide the most complete picture of any given language.

That languages change is obvious to anyone familiar with more archaic literature. In the case of English, one need look no further than the early Modern English found in the King James Bible. For example, the

5. Lyle Campbell, *Historical Linguistics: An Introduction* (Cambridge: MIT Press, 1999), xii–xv, 1–5.

King James equivalents of the Modern English phrases *my affliction* and *my house* are *mine affliction* and *mine house*, respectively, even though a Modern English phrase like *my time* also corresponds with *my time* in the King James. This is because, in this earlier form of English, the 1CSG possessive pronoun ended with the nasal /n/ before words beginning with vowels and *h*. Over time, partly for phonological reasons,[6] the form *my* eventually replaced *mine* before vowels and *h* as well. This is just one of many examples that could be cited.

Language change happens in all languages that are spoken and generally becomes more significant as time progresses. While change can happen in all realms of a language (e.g., syntax, morphology, lexicon), we are primarily concerned with language change in the realm of phonology, which can be referred to as **sound change**. There are many different types or classifications of sound changes in historical linguistics. Most broadly, sound change may be classified as "regular" or "sporadic," the former referring to changes that happen more or less as a rule, and the latter to changes that do not occur consistently throughout the language. Sound change can further be classified as "unconditioned" or "conditioned," the former referring to changes that occur without exception, and the latter to changes that occur in particular phonological environments. Finally, sound change may be either "phonemic" or "nonphonemic," depending on whether it affects the phonemic realization of a given sound or merely its allophones (see §3.3).[7] Moreover, as languages change over time, it is often the case that a phonetic change can precipitate an eventual phonemic change. In many instances, a wide-reaching sound change begins only in a "highly localized context" and then gradually spreads.[8]

Within these above classifications, there are many types of changes that may occur, such as mergers, splits, assimilation, dissimilation, epen-

---

6. Cf. Campbell, *Historical Linguistics*, 9.

7. Campbell, *Historical Linguistics*, 16–19.

8. Richard D. Janda and Brian D. Joseph, "Reconsidering the Canons of Sound-Change: Towards a 'Big Bang' Theory," in *Historical Linguistics 2001: Selected Papers from the 15th International Conference on Historical Linguistics, Melbourne, 13–17 August 2001*, ed. Barry J. Blake and Kate Burridge (Amsterdam/Philadelphia: John Benjamins, 2003), 206.

thesis, etc. Because it lies beyond the scope of this section to present them all here,[9] it is recommended that the reader consult an introduction to the field of historical linguistics, such as Lyle Campbell's *Historical Linguistics: An Introduction* (chapters 1–2), where all the relevant sound changes are covered with instructive and easy-to-understand examples.[10] If not familiar with such phenomena, the reader would do well to consult this work—or to use it as a reference—while reading the rest of this book.

9. A highly abbreviated summary of the most important types of sound change follows. A **merger** occurs when two distinct sounds merge into one, whereas a **split** occurs when one distinct sound splits into two. **Assimilation** involves one sound coming to be pronounced more similarly to another nearby sound, whereas **dissimilation** involves one sound coming to be pronounced more dissimilarly from another nearby (and similar) sound. **Deletion** refers to the loss of a particular sound in a word, whereas **epenthesis** refers to the secondary insertion of an additional sound into a word. **Excrescence** is a type of epenthesis that involves the insertion of a consonant (usually between two other consonants) often used to facilitate pronunciation. **Compensatory lengthening** occurs when one sound drops out and another sound comes to be pronounced longer to make up for it. **Metathesis** refers to the transposition of two sounds. **Voicing** refers to a consonant pronounced without vibration of the vocal cords coming to be pronounced with such vibration, whereas **devoicing** refers to the opposite. **Palatalization** involves a velar or alveolar sound coming to be pronounced more in the region of the palate (palato-alveolar). **Monophthongization** involves the contraction of a diphthong sound to a single vowel. **Vowel raising** is the change of a vowel to one higher on the axis, whereas **vowel lowering** is the reverse. **Gemination** refers to the "doubling" (or extending the duration) of a consonant, whereas **degemination** refers to the opposite. **Lengthening** and **shortening** refer to the same process but in the case of vowels. For detailed explanations and examples, see Campbell, *Historical Linguistics*, 19–48.

10. Campbell, *Historical Linguistics*, 1–56.

4

How Was Koine Greek
Pronounced Historically?

The historical pronunciation of New Testament Greek is outlined below letter-by-letter (or grapheme-by-grapheme), divided into consonants, diphthongs, and vowels. The comprehensive analysis of the Judeo-Palestinian epigraphic and documentary material presented in *PNTG* is what ultimately underlies the reconstructed pronunciation outlined below. In each section, after a brief explanation of how to pronounce the relevant sound/letter, several Greek examples are cited with IPA phonemic and phonetic transcription. Following this, the most pertinent evidence from the Judeo-Palestinian material for each pronunciation and/or phonological development is summarized. Because Judeo-Palestinian Greek was but one of many regional varieties of the Koine spoken at the time of the New Testament, each section concludes with an "Around the Mediterranean" explanatory box, which surveys the linguistic diversity attested in the Koine-speaking world elsewhere in the Mediterranean. Readers will thus be able to gain a fairly accurate picture of the pronunciation of Koine Greek at the time of the New Testament not just in Judea-Palestine but around the Mediterranean as well. In this way, this short volume will indeed familiarize readers with the "pronunciation of New Testament Greek" in all its diversity.

It should also be noted that the pronunciation system outlined in this book is that of the more "common" register characteristic of everyday speech rather than of poetry, songs, or speeches (see §4.3.8). If one had to name the pronunciation system recommended in this book, "Common Koine" or "Everyday Koine" might be the best moniker. As described in the larger volume (see, e.g., *PNTG* §§8.3.2.1.I; 8.6.1), a careful analysis of the material leads to the conclusion that multiple pronunciation systems existed in the first century CE. There was a more conservative register, which maintained linguistic features like vocalic length, and a more innovative register, which had neutralized features like vowel length. Although we cannot be sure about the exact distribution of these pronunciation systems at the time of the New Testament, there is some evidence that the conservative system was more common in formal contexts (poems, songs, speeches, official communication, etc.) and the innovative system was more common in less formal contexts (everyday communication, at home, in the marketplace, etc.) (see *PNTG* §9.2). As such, given the pedagogical purposes of this volume, we present below the pronunciation system of the more "common" or "everyday speech" register.

In some cases, there may be changes that were still in flux during the first century CE and were not stabilized until the second century CE, such as the merger of αι, ε → ε and οι, υ → υ (see *PNTG* §8.2.1–2). For such cases, I opt for the pronunciation that obtained after the stabilization of the development. This is not necessarily to say that the pronunciation did not exist in the first century CE, but merely that there was diversity among different portions of the population. Perhaps the most extended application of this principle concerns the realization of the historical stops χ, φ, θ, and δ, which were probably pronounced as [kʰ], [pʰ], [tʰ], and [d] in first-century Judea-Palestine. Although there is evidence that these sounds had become fricatives for some speakers by the end of the Roman period (3rd/4th c. CE), it is not entirely clear how early the fricativization of these consonants occurred. Nevertheless, because this process was already underway during the Roman period—and because it has pedagogical advantages—I recommend that readers of the New Testament pronounce all the historical stops as they would have been pronounced when the development was complete, namely as the fricatives [x], [ɸ], [θ], and [ð]. At the same time, there may also be evidence that, at least for a time, the fricative pronunciations were considered more "colloquial" and the stop pronunciations more "formal" or "high register."[1] A fricative pronunciation is thus consistent with my goal of presenting the "Common Koine" or "Everyday Koine" pronunciation.

On this point, it should also be noted that there is a difference in the nature of evidence for changes in the vowel system as opposed to changes in the consonantal system. When the pronunciation of a vowel changes, it often encroaches on (or even merges with) another vowel in the vowel space. As a result, spelling interchanges are quite common and often begin to be attested immediately after the change. When the pronunciation of a consonant changes, on the other hand, it can often do so without necessarily becoming more similar to any other consonants in the system. As a result, the orthography only very rarely indicates a change in the pronunciation of a consonant. Because of this, many of the examples cited in this section to illustrate changes in the consonantal system of Judeo-Palestinian Greek come from the Byzantine period. While in some cases this chronological distribution is meaningful, in other cases it may simply be an accident of statistics. There is more than twice as much material from the Byzantine period as there is from the Roman period and more than ten times as much material from the Byzantine period as there is from the first century CE. Therefore, just because examples to illustrate changes in the consonantal system are dated to the Byzantine period does not mean that these changes did not apply earlier. The historical depth of a consonantal change that is attested only in the Byzantine period can sometimes be clarified in light of loanword evidence (Greek loanwords in Rabbinic Hebrew) and comparative material from other regional varieties of the Koine.

While the time of the composition of the New Testament, namely the latter part of the first century CE, is the intended timeframe for the reconstructed pronunciation presented below, one cannot fully appreciate the pronunciation of first-century Greek without also considering the pronunciation of Greek leading up to and following this century. As such, when discussing the pronunciation of New Testament Greek, I will often refer to various time periods, both before and after the first century,

---

1. See James Clackson, "A Greek Papyrus in Armenian Script," *Zeitschrift für Papyrologie und Epigraphik* 129 (2000): 251–52.

so that readers can gain a sense of the history and/or trajectory of a particular development. In particular, these time periods are the Hellenistic period (332–37 BCE), the early Roman period (37 BCE–135 CE), the late Roman period (135–324 CE), and the Byzantine period (324–638 CE).

Finally, because the reconstructed pronunciation outlined here is ultimately based on the research presented in the larger volume (*PNTG*), cross-references to the corresponding sections in *PNTG* are included in each of the letter headings. Moreover, where appropriate, cross-references to *PNTG* are also included in the commentary and discussion on each sound. In this way, those who are interested in finding out more about the evidence relevant for reconstructing a particular sound can quickly and easily utilize *PNTG* as a reference.

4.1 CONSONANTS

4.1.1 γ (PNTG §7.1.1)

Generally, the consonant γ is pronounced like a "soft" *g*, that is, like English *g* but with continuing airflow. This is called a voiced velar fricative (IPA /ɣ/).

γάμος	/ɣámos/	[ˈɣɑmo̞s]
γράφω	/ɣráɸo/	[ˈɣrɑɸo̞]
λόγος	/lóɣos/	[ˈlo̞ɣo̞s]

Before front vowels, namely ι–ει, υ–οι, η–ηι (η), ε–αι, this "soft" *g* sound is pronounced by moving the body of the tongue slightly more forward on the palate so that it sounds almost like a "tight" *y* with continued airflow (for more on how to pronounce palatalized consonants, see §4.1.8). This sound, which is considered an allophone of γ = /ɣ/, is called a voiced palatal fricative (IPA [ʝ]).

γείνεσθαι	/ɣínesθe/	[ˈʝine̞sθe̞]
ἐγένετο	/eɣéneto/	[e̞ˈʝe̞ne̞to̞]
λόγοι	/lóɣy/	[ˈlo̞ʝy]

The fricativization and palatalization of γ is evidenced in the Judeo-Palestinian Greek material by the γ → ι spelling interchange attested in a late Roman inscription from Beth She'arim: ιη (for γῆ) (BETH0168, 3rd–4th c. CE) (see *PNTG* §7.1.1.1.I). Greek loanwords in Hebrew also reflect the pronunciation γ = /ɣ, j/. In two Hebrew texts from the Roman period, the emperor Trajan's name is spelled as טרוגיינוס/טרוגינוס (ṬRWGYYNWS/ṬRWGYNWS), which possibly reflects a slavishly literal copying of the Greek orthography τραγ(ε)ιανος (for τραϊανός). If this is the case, it would indicate that γ represented a palatal fricative [j] before front (high?) vowels (see *PNTG* §7.1.1.4.V). Though considerably later, in late Samaritan Aramaic the word γένεσις is rendered as אנסיס (ʔNSYS), עניסוס (ʕNYSWS), and ניסוס (NYSWS), which also indicates that γ was pronounced as a palatal fricative [j] before front vowels (see *PNTG* §7.1.1.4.VI). Although this evidence is later than the first century CE, taken all together it likely indicates that γ had already become palatalized by the first century, especially in light of comparative material from other regional varieties of Koine.

γ around the Mediterranean

At the time of the New Testament, it is probable that γ was pronounced as /ɣ, j/ in most regional varieties of the Koine. The fricativization (and palatalization) of γ was a relatively early change in the consonantal system across the Mediterranean. It is evidenced in Egypt already from early in the Hellenistic period in spellings like υγιγαινει (for ὑγιαίνει) (*SB* 4.7402.18, ca. 250 BCE) and ιγερεων (for ἱερέων) (*BGU* 4.1198.4, 4 BCE), in which a superfluous γ is added before a front vowel.[2] It is also attested in Greece at an early date, but not necessarily in the same environment. Second-century BCE Attic spellings like ολιον (for ὀλίγον) may indicate that γ passed to [j] in this environment. There are, however, more widely comparable examples from Attica, like ιγερων (for ἱερων-) dated to the Hellenistic period.[3] Anatolian inscriptions of the Roman period also exhibit likely fricativization and

2. Sven-Tage Teodorsson, *The Phonology of Ptolemaic Koine* (Göteborg: Acta Universitatis Gothoburgensis, 1977), 187.

3. Leslie Threatte, *The Grammar of Attic Inscriptions I: Phonology* (Berlin: de Gruyter, 1980), 440–41.

palatalization before front vowels: e.g., ιδιοπραεων (for ιδιοπραγέων) and συν τυς υγυς (for σὺν τοῖς υἱοῖς).[4] The evidence from Italy is not entirely clear, but late Roman examples like γιερουσαρχη, ιερουσιαρχη[ς], and ειεροσαρχης (probably for γερουσιάρχης) may reflect γ = /y, j/.[5]

After a nasal consonant, namely in the sequences (γ)γ or (ν)γ, the normal "hard" stop pronunciation of γ (like regular English *g*) is maintained. This sound, which may be considered an allophone of γ = /ɣ/,[6] is called a voiced velar stop (IPA [g]).

σπόγγος	/spónyos/	[ˈspɔ(ŋ)gɔs]
φέγγος	/ɸényos/	[ˈɸɛ(ŋ)gɔs]
ἀγγαρεύω	/anyaréβo/	[a(ŋ)gaˈrɛβɔ]

4. Claude Brixhe, *Essai sur le grec anatolien au début de notre ère* (Nancy: Presses Universitaires de Nancy, 1987), 39–40.

5. Note, however, that such spellings might have been influenced by the more common ἱερός or ἱερεύς. Further, instances of Latin *c* for Greek γ and vice versa may provide counterevidence. See Harry Joshua Leon, "The Language of the Greek Inscriptions from the Jewish Catacombs of Rome," *Transactions and Proceedings of the American Philological Association* 58 (1927): 226–27.

6. There may be different ways to interpret such sequences phonemically. One could argue that the phoneme was actually still /g/ generally, the pronunciation of which was preserved after nasals, and that both [ɣ] and [j] were allophones. This would be a more "archaic" phonemic analysis and might apply if fricativization and palatalization of γ was still early in development and not yet totally stable. On the other hand, because voicing after nasals rendered κ and γ identical in this environment, one might also suggest that a post-nasal γ always represents the phoneme /k/, which had allophones of [g] and [j] in this environment. This is one possible phonemic analysis of Modern Greek: e.g., αγγούρι 'cucumber' = /ankúri/ [a(ŋ)ˈguri]; άγγελος 'angel' = /ánkelos/ [ˈa(ɲ)ɟelɔs]. See David Holton, Peter Mackridge, and Irene Philippaki-Warburton, *Greek: A Comprehensive Grammar* (New York: Routledge, 2012), 5. Such a phonemic analysis could be applied to Koine Greek, but it might be the case that only Modern Greek permits such an analysis since it had so much time to stabilize and reconfigure after certain phonological developments and mergers. Given the variation and instability of some of these changes during the Koine period, it seems preferable to posit a middle ground: i.e., phoneme /ɣ/ with allophones [g], [ɟ], and [j]. A similar principle applies in the case of post-nasal β and δ (see footnotes 22 and 30).

After a nasal consonant + before front vowels, namely in the sequences (γ)γ or (ν)γ followed by ι–ει, υ–οι, η–ηι (η), ε–αι, the "hard" stop *g* sound is also palatalized. It is pronounced like the palatalized γ before front vowels as outlined above, but with the airflow stopped instead of continuing. This sound, which is considered an allophone of γ = /ɣ/, is called a voiced palatal stop (IPA [ɟ]) (note that the preceding nasal also becomes palatalized here [see further below]).

ἄγγελος	/ánɣelos/	[ˈa(ɲ)ɟelo̞s]
ἐγγύς	/enɣýs/	[ε(ɲ)ˈɟys]
ἐγγίζειν	/enɣízin/	[ε(ɲ)ˈɟizin]

There is no explicit evidence in the Judeo-Palestinian material for the preserved stop pronunciation of γ after a nasal. Nevertheless, the fact that there is explicit evidence for the preserved stop pronunciation of both β and δ after a nasal in Judeo-Palestinian (see §§4.1.2; 4.1.3) makes it highly likely that the same applied in the case of γ.

(γ)γ, (ν)γ around the Mediterranean

A continued stop pronunciation of γ following a nasal may be evidenced in the interchanges γγ → γκ and γκ → γγ/νγ attested in the Egyptian papyri: e.g., αγκελλις (for ἀγγέλλεις) (P.Princ. 2.66, 1st c. CE) and ενγαλο (for ἐγκαλῶ) (Stud.Pal. 22.46, 2nd c. CE).[7] At the same time, however, interchanges of γ and κ are common in Egyptian Greek in all environments due to bilingual interference from Coptic.[8] There is no direct evidence in the Koine period for the palatalization of the "hard" stop pronunciation after nasal consonants. However, given the general evidence for the palatalization of velar consonants before front vowels (see §4.1.8), we may be reasonably confident that it applied in these sorts of contexts as well.

---

7. Search via the TM Text Irregularities database. See Mark Depauw and Joanne Stolk, "Linguistic Variation in Greek Papyri: Towards a New Tool for Quantitative Study," *Greek, Roman, and Byzantine Studies* 55 (2015).

8. Francis Thomas Gignac, *A Grammar of the Greek Papyri of the Roman and Byzantine Periods*, vol. 1, *Phonology* (Milan: Istituto Editoriale Cisalpino, 1976), 76–80.

Before velar consonants, namely γ, κ, χ, ξ, the consonant γ is pronounced through the nose (i.e., nasal) like *ng* in the English word *sing*. This is called a voiced velar nasal (IPA [ŋ]). In most cases, it is best considered an allophone of ν = /n/ rather than γ = /ɣ/. There was also a significant tendency for this sound to be weakened before a stop consonant so that it was not pronounced at all or left behind a slight nasal quality on the preceding vowel. This weakness is signified by putting the sound in parentheses as [(ŋ)] in the phonetic transcription.

σάλπιγγα	/sálpinɣa/	[ˈsalpi(ŋ)ga]
συγκαλεῖν	/synkalín/	[sy(ŋ)gaˈlin]
τυγχάνω	/tynxáno/	[tyŋˈxano̞]

Before palatalized velar consonants, namely in the sequences γ(γ), γ(κ), γ(χ) followed by ι–ει, υ–οι, η–ηι (η), ε–αι, this velar nasal is pronounced slightly more forward on the palate. In other words, it is pronounced just like [ɟ] above but with airflow going through the nose instead of stopping. This is called a voiced palatal nasal (IPA [ɲ]). If one is careful to palatalize the following velar, palatalization of the preceding nasal follows naturally. Like the previous sound, it is usually considered an allophone of ν = /n/ and exhibits weakness before the stop consonant [ɟ].

σάλπιγγι	/sálpinyi/	[ˈsalpi(ɲ)ɟi]
ἀνάγκη	/anánke/	[aˈna(ɲ)ɟe]
ἐλέγχειν	/elénxin/	[eˈleɲçin]

In Judea-Palestine, it was actually significantly more common for scribes working in the first century CE to spell "standard" γγ, γκ, γξ, γχ with an initial ν as νγ, νκ, νξ, νχ: e.g., ενγυς (for ἐγγύς) (8HevXIIgr, 50 BCE–50 CE); μετενενκη (for μετενέγκη) (*CIIP* 385, 1–70 CE); λυνξ (for λύγξ) (*CIIP* 3568, Hellenistic); εντυνχανω (for ἐντυγχάνω) (5/6Hev34, 131 CE). For more on this phenomenon as a particularly "Roman" feature, see *PNTG* §7.1.1.2. The palatalization of the velar nasal γ(γ) is not explicitly evidenced in the ancient material. Nevertheless, given the evidence for the palatalization of velar consonants before front vowels (see §4.1.8), it is phonetically likely that a velar nasal [ŋ] would be palatalized to [ɲ] in such an environment (i.e., before [j]or [ç]).

γγ, γκ, γξ, γχ and νγ, νκ, νξ, νχ around the Mediterranean

At the time of the New Testament, most scribes around the Mediterranean were probably writing νγ, νκ, νξ, νχ (i.e., unassimilated forms) instead of the "standard" sequences γγ, γκ, γξ, γχ (i.e., assimilated forms) in most words. In Attic inscriptions, while there is considerable variation in the Hellenistic period, there is a clear preference for unassimilated forms in the Roman period: e.g., συνκλη- (for συγκλη-) (85–95 CE); ενκαλω (for ἐγκαλῶ) (162–163 CE).[9] In the Egyptian material, there are some instances of ενκ- (for εγκ-) and συνκ- (for συγκ-) in the Hellenistic period, but there is a noticeable increase beginning in the first century BCE/CE: e.g., ενγυς (for ἐγγύς) (*SB* 20.14242, 1st c. CE).[10] In Anatolia, unassimilated forms are quite common in the Roman period, though traditional spellings can be more prevalent in areas with a greater tie to past Hellenization (e.g., Pontus).[11] In Italy, assimilation is rare in the second- and third-century CE Jewish catacombs of Rome; most forms are written unassimilated: e.g., ενκωμια (for ἐγκώμια).[12]

Before the bilabial nasal, namely in the sequence γ(μ), the consonant γ is pronounced as a velar nasal [ŋ] like its pronunciation before velar consonants (see above). In such cases, however, it is considered an allophone of /ɣ/ rather than of /n/ as in the sequences γ(γ), γ(κ), etc.[13]

πρᾶγμα	/práɣma/	[ˈpraŋma]
διωγμός	/ðioɣmós/	[ðjoŋˈmos]
κήρυγμα	/kéryɣma/	[ˈceryŋma]

---

9. Threatte, *Grammar of Attic Inscriptions I*, 588–616.

10. Search via the TM Text Irregularities database. See Depauw and Stolk, "Linguistic Variation."

11. Brixhe, *Grec anatolien*, 34, 36.

12. Leon, "Jewish Catacombs," 229–30.

13. For references to this sound in the ancient Greek grammarians, see W. Sidney Allen, *Vox Graeca: A Guide to the Pronunciation of Classical Greek* (Cambridge: Cambridge University Press, 1968), 35.

There is no explicit evidence for this pronunciation in the Judeo-Palestinian Greek material, but it is plausible based on comparative evidence.

γμ around the Mediterranean

At the time of the New Testament, while there is limited evidence, it is plausible that Koine Greek speakers partially assimilated γ to a following μ and pronounced the sequence γμ as [ŋm]. In Egyptian papyri of the late Roman period, the sequence γμ sometimes interchanges with μμ: e.g., πραμμα (for πρᾶγμα) (*SB* 24.16269, 3rd c. CE; P.Sakaon. 39, 318 CE).[14] The same is attested in Roman-period inscriptions from Anatolia: e.g., σιμμα (for σῖγμα).[15] The fact that the velar nasal [ŋ] was called ἄγμα by the ancient grammarians also supports this point.[16]

4.1.2 β (PNTG §7.1.2)

Generally, the consonant β is pronounced like a "soft" *b* sound, in between that of English *b* and *v*. For those who know Spanish, a better comparison would be the Spanish *b* and *v* sounds in words like *sabes* [ˈsaβes] 'you know' or *favor* [faˈβor] 'favor'. This sound is made with the lips together as if one were going to pronounce English *b* but by letting the airflow continue. This is called a voiced bilabial fricative (IPA /β/).

βασιλεύς	/basiléφs/	[βaṣiˈleφs]
λάβε	/lábe/	[ˈlaβe]
βιβλίον	/bíblíon/	[βiˈβlịon]

---

14. Search via the TM Text Irregularities database. See Depauw and Stolk, "Linguistic Variation."

15. Brixhe, *Grec anatolien*, 39.

16. See Threatte, *Grammar of Attic Inscriptions I*, 583–84 and Edgar H. Sturtevant, *The Pronunciation of Greek and Latin* (Chicago: Ares, 1940), 64.

In Modern Greek, β is pronounced as a voiced labiodental fricative like English *v* (IPA /v/). The subtle shift of β = /β/ to /v/ probably occurred during the Byzantine period. For those who find /β/ difficult, pronouncing /v/ is a reasonable substitute.

βασιλεύς	/vasiléfs/	[vɑsiˈlɛfs]
λάβε	/láve/	[ˈlavɛ̱]
βιβλίον	/vivlíon/	[viˈvlio̱n]

In the Judeo-Palestinian Greek material, the fricativization of β appears to be reflected already in the Hellenistic period in the following spelling: αυδοκωσου (for ἀβδοκώσου) (*CIIP* 3635, 2nd/1st c. BCE) (*PNTG* §7.1.2.1.I). There are also some instances in which Greek β is rendered with Hebrew *vav* ו (w or v) in loanwords in the Mishnah: e.g., λέσβιον → ליזוויז (LYZVYZ); βῆλον → וילן (VYLWN) (*PNTG* §7.1.2.3.IV–V). Greek transcriptions of Latin consonantal *v* with β might also be relevant here: e.g., βερουταριου (for Latin *Verutarius*) (*CIIP* 221–222, 1st c. BCE/CE). However, the interpretation of such evidence is less clear (*PNTG* §7.10.1.2.IV).

β around the Mediterranean

At the time of the New Testament, most regional varieties of the Koine realized Greek β as a bilabial fricative [β]. The fricativization of β likely took place by the first century BCE or the first century CE in the majority of Koine dialects. In Egypt, aside from the second-century BCE spelling ραυδους (for ράβδους) (*UPZ* 1.12, 1.13, 2nd c. BCE),[17] evidence for the fricativization of β begins in the first century CE with spellings like πνευτυνις (for πνεβτύνι) (P.Mich. 5.263, 35/36 CE).[18] In Asia Minor, a fricative β is reflected by the first century CE in Miletos and by the second century CE in Magnesia.[19] By the late Roman period, a fricative β appears to be the norm in

---

17. Search via the TM Text Irregularities database. See Depauw and Stolk, "Linguistic Variation."

18. Teodorsson, *Ptolemaic Koine*, 238; Gignac, *Grammar of the Greek Papyri I*, 68–71.

19. Vit Bubenik, *Hellenistic and Roman Greece as a Sociolinguistic Area* (Amsterdam/Philadelphia: John Benjamins, 1989), 245.

Anatolian Koine: e.g., αναπαβετε (for ἀναπαύεται).[20] The evidence in Greece and Italy is more ambiguous. In both the Attic inscriptions and the catacombs of Rome, one might interpret the use of Greek β to represent Latin *v* in names like φλαβια (for *Flavia*) as evidence for the fricativization of Greek β, but it is just as plausible that a stop [b] could be the nearest Greek equivalent of Latin *v* = [β] or [v].[21]

After a nasal consonant, namely in the sequences (μ)β or (ν)β, the normal "hard" stop pronunciation of β (like regular English *b*) is maintained. This sound, which is an allophone of β = /β/,[22] is called a voiced bilabial stop (IPA [b]).

λαμβάνω	/lamβáno/	[la(m)'banǫ]
ἔμβολος	/énβolos/	['ɛ(m)bǫlǫs]
σύνβιος	/sýnβios/	['sy(n)bjǫs]

In the Judeo-Palestinian material, the stop pronunciation of β following a nasal consonant is evidenced through Byzantine spellings like σαμβατου (for σαββάτου) (ZOOR0131, 427 CE) and λαμβρο(τατω) (for λαμπρο(τάτῳ)) (P Ness 3 26, 570 CE) (*PNTG* §§7.1.2.2.I; 7.4.2.2.I). Because the stop pronunciation of β in this environment is a retention rather than an innovation, such Byzantine spellings imply that β following a nasal was pronounced as a stop in earlier periods as well. This is further supported by the rendering of the sequence μβ as geminated ב /bb/ in

20. Brixhe, *Grec anatolien*, 39, 57–58; Claude Brixhe, "Linguistic Diversity in Asia Minor during the Empire: *Koine* and Non-Greek Languages," in *A Companion to the Ancient Greek Language*, ed. Egbert J. Bakker (Malden: Wiley-Blackwell, 2010), 234–35.

21. Leon, "Jewish Catacombs," 227; Threatte, *Grammar of Attic Inscriptions I*, 442–47.

22. Other phonemic interpretations of such sequences may be possible. We could posit a general phoneme /b/, which has an allophone [β] when not following a nasal consonant. Alternatively, because voicing after nasals rendered π and β identical in this environment, one might also suggest that a post-nasal β always represents the phoneme /p/, which had the allophone [b] in this environment. The same principle may apply in the case of post-nasal γ and δ as well (see footnotes 6 and 30). In light of inconsistency in the Koine, however, I have opted for a middle ground: phoneme /β/ with allophone [b].

Greek loanwords in Rabbinic Hebrew: e.g., אַבּוּל /ʔibbul/ (for ἔμβολος) (*PNTG* §7.1.2.3.VI).

μβ around the Mediterranean

That β continued to be pronounced as a stop after nasal consonants may be evidenced in the interchanges μβ → μπ and μπ → μβ attested in the Egyptian papyri: e.g., εμπηναι (for ἐμβῆναι) (P.Oxy. 295.6, ca. 35 CE); εμβροστεν (for ἔμπροσθεν) (P.Ryl.Gr. 2.174a, 2nd c. CE); κραμπην (for κράμβης) (O.Krok. 1.97, 2nd c. CE).[23] As noted earlier, however, interchanges between voiced and voiceless stops are common in Egyptian Greek due to bilingual interference from Coptic.[24]

4.1.3 δ (PNTG §7.1.3)

Pedagogically, the consonant δ is pronounced like a voiced *th* sound as in the English word *this*. This is called a voiced interdental fricative (IPA /ð/).

δοῦλος	/ðúlos/	[ˈðulọs]
οἶδα	/ýða/	[ˈyða]
καρδία	/karðía/	[karˈðia]

Historically,[25] the consonant δ was probably still pronounced like the letter *d* in the English word *dog* in the first century. This is called a voiced alveolar stop (IPA /d/).

---

23. Search via the TM Text Irregularities database. See Depauw and Stolk, "Linguistic Variation." See also Gignac, *Grammar of the Greek Papyri I*, 76–80.

24. Gignac, *Grammar of the Greek Papyri I*, 83–86.

25. Given the pedagogically-minded choice to recommend the fricative pronunciation of the historically aspirated stops (see footnote 33), it is also natural to recommend the fricative pronunciation of δ, since an authentic historical pronunciation system that had a fricative θ would likely also have had a fricative δ.

δοῦλος	/dúlos/	['dulǫs]
οἶδα	/ýda/	['ydɑ]
καρδία	/kardía/	[kar'diɑ]

In the Judeo-Palestinian material, the earliest evidence for a fricative δ appears to come in the (probably) late Roman inscriptional spellings κωζωνος (for κώδωνος) (*CIIP* 2186, 3rd–5th c. CE) and κοχχαθιων (for κοχαδιων) (*CIIP* 2179, 3rd–6th c. CE) (see *PNTG* §7.1.3.1.I–II). In the second example, the fact that δ interchanges with θ rather than τ likely indicates that it was a fricative and no longer a stop. There is no explicit evidence for a fricative δ in Judeo-Palestinian Greek earlier than the third century CE.

δ around the Mediterranean

At the time of the New Testament, most regional varieties of the Koine probably still pronounced δ as a stop, though it likely had already become a fricative for some speakers. Indeed, while some regional varieties of the Koine attest to the fricativization of δ at an early date, it was likely not widespread until the third or fourth century CE. In the Egyptian papyri, there is sporadic evidence for a fricative δ starting in the first century CE: e.g., εβζωμου (for ἐβδόμου) (P.Soter. 6, 1st c. CE); χορζιν (for χορδήν) (O.Heid. 428, 1st–2nd c. CE); τραπεδειτη (for τραπεζίτη) (P. L.Bat. 1.14, 2nd c. CE); ελπιδω (for ἐλπίζω) (P.Iand. 2.11, 3rd–4th c. CE).[26] Most such examples, however, are dated to the third century CE or later. Anatolian Koine clearly exhibits fricativization of δ by the Roman period: e.g., πλαδιμους (for πλαθιμούς) and βοηδιος (for βοήθιος).[27] In Italy, interchanges like ζαβιου (for διὰ βίου) may reflect a fricative δ already in the late Roman period, but such spellings might also indicate an affricate ζ = [dʒ].[28] There is no clear evidence for the fricativization of δ in Greece during the Roman period.[29]

---

26. Search via the TM Text Irregularities database. See Depauw and Stolk, "Linguistic Variation." See also Gignac, *Grammar of the Greek Papyri I*, 75–76.

27. Brixhe, *Grec anatolien*, 39; Brixhe, "Asia Minor," 234–35.

28. Leon, "Jewish Catacombs," 230. See also Sturtevant, *Pronunciation*, 190.

29. Threatte, *Grammar of Attic Inscriptions I*, 442–47.

After a nasal consonant, namely in the sequence (ν)δ, the normal "hard" stop pronunciation of δ (like regular English *d*) is maintained. This sound, which is an allophone of δ = /ð/,[30] is called a voiced alveolar stop (IPA [d]).

δένδρον	/ðénðron/	['ðɛ(n)drọn]
ἄνδρα	/ánðra/	['a(n)dra]
σκάνδαλον	/skánðalon/	['ṣka(n)dalọn]

In the Judeo-Palestinian material, the stop pronunciation of δ following a nasal is clearly demonstrated by the Byzantine spelling φανενδος (for φανέντος) (*CIIP* Ap.18, 6th c. CE or later) (*PNTG* §7.4.3.2.I). As noted earlier regarding β, because the post-nasal stop pronunciation of δ is a retention and not an innovation, Byzantine evidence for a stop pronunciation after nasals implies that it was realized as a stop in this environment in earlier periods as well. This is likely also reflected in the earlier inscriptional spelling ιερον τρυφακτου (for ἱερὸν δρυφάκτου) (*CIIP* 2, 23 BCE–70 CE) (*PNTG* §7.1.3.2.I).

νδ around the Mediterranean

The fact that δ was pronounced as a stop after nasal consonants may be evidenced in the interchanges νδ → ντ and ντ → νδ attested in the Egyptian papyri: e.g., υπαρχονδα (for ὑπάρχοντα) (P.Ryl.Gr. 2.160c, 32 CE) and τηντε (for τήνδε) (P.Mich. 5 254, 30/31 CE).[31] Since these examples come from Egypt, however, it is always possible that bilingual interference from Cop-

---

30. Other phonemic interpretations of this sequence are possible. One could posit a general phoneme of /d/, which has an allophone [ð] when not following a nasal consonant. Alternatively, because voicing after nasals rendered τ and δ identical in this environment, one might also suggest that a post-nasal δ always represents the phoneme /t/, which had the allophone [d]. The same principle applies for post-nasal γ and β as well (see footnotes 6 and 22). Because of inconsistency and lack of stability during the Koine period, however, I have opted for a middle ground: phoneme /ð/ with allophone [d].

31. Search via the TM Text Irregularities database. See Depauw and Stolk, "Linguistic Variation." See also Gignac, *Grammar of the Greek Papyri I*, 80–83.

tic is a factor. The evidence from Anatolian Koine is thus perhaps more transparent: e.g., δεκαπενδε (for δεκαπέντε).[32]

4.1.4 χ (PNTG §7.2.1)

Pedagogically, the consonant χ should be pronounced like a "soft" *k*, that is, like English *k* but with continuing airflow instead of a stop. While some introductory textbooks compare the sound of χ to the *ch* sound in *Bach*, this is unhelpful. The sound *ch* in the word *Bach* is a uvular fricative, pronounced more in the throat, whereas Greek χ is pronounced further forward (i.e., like *k* but with continued airflow). It is pronounced in the same place as the primary pronunciation of γ (IPA /ɣ/) but without vibrating the vocal cords. Indeed, a better comparison than the *ch* in German *Bach* would be the *j* sound in Spanish *ojos* = ['oxos] 'eyes'. This sound is called a voiceless velar fricative (IPA /x/).

χριστός	/xristós/	[xri'st̥o̥s]
χάρις	/xáris/	['xɑris̥]
ἔχω	/éxo/	['ɛxo̥]

Historically,[33] the consonant χ was probably still pronounced as an aspirated *k* sound in the first century, much like the pronunciation of English *c* in the word *cat*. This sound is called an aspirated voiceless velar stop (IPA /kʰ/).

---

32. Brixhe, *Grec anatolien*, 34–37; Brixhe, "Asia Minor," 234; Bubenik, *Hellenistic and Roman Greece*, 239.

33. The pronunciation of the historical aspirated stops, namely χ, φ, θ, is one of the few places where the pronunciation outlined here differs from that which was used in Judea-Palestine during the first century CE. Because a distinction between aspirated and unaspirated stops is difficult for many modern learners of Koine Greek, I have opted to use the slightly later (late Roman or early Byzantine) fricative pronunciation of χ, φ, θ as [x], [ɸ], [θ] instead of the first-century CE aspirated pronunciation of χ, φ, θ as [kʰ], [pʰ], [tʰ].

χριστός   /kʰristós/   [kʰriˈsto̞s]

χάρις   /kʰáris/   [ˈkʰaris̞]

ἔχω   /ékʰo/   [ˈɛkʰo̞]

In the Judeo-Palestinian Greek material, possible evidence for this change occurs in the representation of Greek χ in loanwords in Hebrew. In some cases, even when immediately following a consonant, Greek χ is rendered into Hebrew by *kaph rafa* כ ([x] or [χ]): e.g., λόγχη → לוֹנְבִּיוֹת (lonχi(-yoθ)). Because Hebrew *kaph* כ (/k, x/ or /k, χ/) was realized as [kʰ] normally (*kaph degusha*) but as [x] (or [χ]) post-vocalically (*kaph rafa*), the use of *kaph rafa* כ ([x] or [χ]) immediately following a consonant may indicate that Greek χ had already become a fricative. However, because this is part of the vocalization of the Mishnah and not the consonantal text, it is possible that this reflects a later Byzantine layer of tradition (see *PNTG* §7.2.1.2.II).

χ around the Mediterranean

At the time of the New Testament, there is not enough evidence to determine which regional varieties (if any) were already pronouncing Greek χ as a fricative [x] instead of an aspirated stop [kʰ]. Some scholars have argued that Anatolian Koine exhibited a fricative χ already in the Roman period, but this may simply come down to assuming a fricative χ in light of the evidence for a fricative φ and θ.[34] It is probable, but by no means certain, that most varieties of the Koine maintained an aspirated stop pronunciation of χ as [kʰ] in the first century. The earliest explicit evidence for a fricative pronunciation of χ actually occurs in the Septuagint translation of the

---

34. Schweizer has argued that the interchanges of χ with κχ, χκ, χχ (e.g., μετηλλακχοτα for μετηλλαχότα) are evidence of a fricative χ, but this is by no means the only interpretation of such interchanges. See Eduard Schweizer, *Grammatik der pergamenischen Inschriften: Beiträge zur Laut- und Flexionslehre der gemeingriechischen Sprache* (Berlin: Weidmannsche Buchandlung, 1898), 114–15. Brixhe, when commenting on Roman Anatolian Koine, explicitly states that "even if there is no clear clue for X, it is probable that the phoneme represented by this sign has undergone the same development [of the fricativization of stops], i.e., /ç/ before /e, i/ and /x/ before /a, o, u/." See Brixhe, "Asia Minor," 235.

Hebrew acrostic in the book of Lamentations as it appears in Codex Vaticanus (early 4th c. CE), where the Hebrew letter names /reːʃ/ and /ʃen/ are
transcribed as ῥήχς and χσέν, respectively (fol. 1134–1139). The transcription
convention χσ for /ʃ/ makes sense only if χ had already shifted to a fricative
[x] but not if it was realized as an aspirated stop [kʰ] (see *PNTG* §7.2.1.4.I).[35]

Pedagogically, before front vowels, namely ι–ει, υ–οι, η–ηι (η), ε–αι,
the fricative χ sound (IPA /x/) is pronounced slightly more forward on
the palate so that it sounds almost like a sort of "hissing" sound (for more
on how to pronounce palatalized consonants, see §4.1.8). This sound,
which is an allophone of χ = /x/, is called a voiceless palatal fricative
(IPA [ç]).

χαῖρε	/xére/	[ˈçɛrɛ]
οὐχί	/uxí/	[uˈçi]
ψυχή	/psyxé/	[ps̬yˈçe]

Historically,[36] before front vowels, namely ι–ει, υ–οι, η–ηι (η), ε–αι,
the χ sound, which was likely still aspirated (IPA /kʰ/) in the first century,
was probably pronounced slightly more forward on the palate, similar to
the pronunciation of *k* in the English word *key*. This sound, which would
be an allophone of χ = /kʰ/, is called an aspirated voiceless palatal stop
(IPA [cʰ]).

χαῖρε	/kʰére/	[ˈcʰɛrɛ]
οὐχί	/ukʰí/	[uˈcʰi]
ψυχή	/psykʰé/	[ps̬yˈcʰe]

There is no explicit evidence in the Judeo-Palestinian material for the
palatal realization of χ before front vowels. Nevertheless, in light of the

35. See also Benjamin Kantor, "The LXX and Historical Greek Phonology: Orthography, Phonology, and Transcriptions," *Journal for the Study of Judaism* 53 (2022): 1–33,
https://doi.org/10.1163/15700631-bja10060.
36. See footnote 33.

general evidence for the palatalization of velar consonants (see §§4.1.1; 4.1.8), it is phonetically plausible that a velar fricative [x] also would have been palatalized to [ç] before front vowels.

χ(ι,υ,η,ε) around the Mediterranean

At the time of the New Testament, there is no explicit evidence for the palatalization of χ, whether as an aspirated stop [cʰ] or as a fricative [ç]. However, the convention of transcribing Hebrew /ʃ/ with Greek χσ in Codex Vaticanus (see above) may indicate that χ had a palatalized allophone of [ç] by the end of the Roman period. Crosslinguistically, [ç] is more likely than [x] to be perceptually associated with [ʃ].[37] In the medieval period, during which the realization of χ as /x, ç/ is well established, Greek χ is used by itself for transcribing Hebrew /ʃ/ when it occurs before front vowels, even though σ is used elsewhere: e.g., βερεχιθ (for בראשית /bereʃiθ/), but cf. ες (for אֶשׁ /ʔeʃ/).[38] Aside from this datum, however, there is no explicit evidence for a palatal allophone of χ before front vowels dated to the Roman period. Nevertheless, given the evidence for the palatalization of the other velars (i.e., γ and x) before front vowels (see §§4.1.1; 4.1.8), it may be reasonably posited that the same principle applied in the case of χ.

4.1.5 φ (PNTG §7.2.2)

Pedagogically, the consonant φ should be pronounced like a "soft" *p* sound, in between that of English *p* and *f*. This sound is made with the lips together as if one were going to pronounce English *p* but by letting the airflow continue. This is called a voiceless bilabial fricative (IPA /ɸ/).

---

37. See discussion of the /ʃ/ → χσ convention in Kantor, "LXX and Phonology."

38. See Benjamin Kantor, "The Thirteenth-Century Hebrew Tradition of the Jews of Southern Italy: Greek Transcriptions of Hebrew Words in Nikolaos of Otranto's 'Disputation against the Jews,'" *Leshonenu* 82, no. 3 (2020): 148–84 [Hebrew].

φωνή	/ɸoné/	[ɸo̞'ne]
προφήτης	/proɸétes/	[pro'ɸetes̠]
φιλεῖ	/ɸilí/	[ɸi'li]

Historically,[39] the consonant φ may still have been pronounced by many speakers in the first century as an aspirated *p* sound, much like the pronunciation of English *p* in the word *pat*. This is called an aspirated voiceless bilabial stop (IPA /pʰ/).[40]

φωνή	/pʰoné/	[pʰo̞'ne]
προφήτης	/propʰétes/	[pro̞'pʰetes]
φιλεῖ	/pʰilí/	[pʰi'li]

In Modern Greek, φ is pronounced as a voiceless labiodental fricative like English *f* (IPA /f/). The subtle shift of φ = /ɸ/ to /f/ probably occurred during the Byzantine period. For those who find /ɸ/ difficult, pronouncing /f/ is a reasonable substitute.

φωνή	/foní/	[fo̞'ni]
προφήτης	/profítis/	[pro̞'fitis]
φιλεῖ	/filí/	[fi'li]

In the Judeo-Palestinian Greek material, there is fairly clear evidence that φ was pronounced as a fricative—at least in the Byzantine period—from the spelling εφυμιας (for εὐφημίας) (*CIIP* 3977, Byzantine). Such

---

39. See footnote 33.

40. Note, however, that if one adopts the more conservative φ = /pʰ/ sound, for the sake of consistency one might also adopt a more conservative pronunciation of the diphthongs αυ and ευ as /au̯/ and /eu̯/ or /aw/ and /ew/. This may be supported by the representation of these sounds in a Greek papyrus written in Armenian script, which appears to reflect the more conservative register. See Clackson, "Greek Papyrus in Armenian." Typologically, the realization of φ and the second element of the diphthongs αυ and ευ should correlate in terms of place of articulation. This also applies if one opts for Modern Greek /f/. Others have noted the phonological correlation of these pronunciations, for which see Ranieri, "Ancient Greek Pronunciation Guide," 24–25.

a spelling is unlikely to occur unless both φ and the υ element in the diphthong ευ were realized as fricatives (see *PNTG* §8.2.5.1.IV). At an earlier period, it is likely that φ was pronounced as an aspirated stop [pʰ]. There is one Hebrew rendering of a Greek loanword in the Mishnah, however, which may indicate a fricative pronunciation already in Roman times: φοῦνδα → אֲפֻנְדְּתוֹ (ʔafundaθo). Because Hebrew *pe* פ (/p, f/ or /p, ɸ/) was realized as a stop [pʰ] normally but as a fricative [f] (or [ɸ]) post-vocalically, the addition of a prothetic *aleph* א (ʔ) to the beginning of this word may be an attempt on the part of the scribe to represent a word-initial fricative φ but according to normal Hebrew sound rules (see *PNTG* §7.2.2.4.IV). It is thus possible that φ was pronounced by some speakers as a stop and by others as a fricative in the Roman period. Typologically, however, the fact that there is fairly clear evidence for the second element of the diphthongs αυ/ευ being pronounced as a bilabial fricative in Roman times (see §4.2.1) may also indicate that φ too had shifted to a fricative by this time.

φ around the Mediterranean

At the time of the New Testament, it is likely that many speakers elsewhere in the Mediterranean were already pronouncing φ as a fricative and that this number was on the rise. Evidence for the fricativization of φ is generally attested sooner than that of χ or θ across the Koine-speaking world. It is reflected in Italy in the first century CE in epigraphic spellings like *dafne* (for δάφνη) found at Pompeii; such a representation in Latin becomes common from the second century CE onward.[41] In Attic inscriptions, Hellenistic- and/or Roman-period spellings like εφρονις (for εὐφρονίς) alongside Latin renderings like *arfocrates* (for ἀρφοκράτης) seem to indicate that φ was already pronounced (at least among a segment of the population) as [ɸ] or [f] in the early Roman period.[42] In South Anatolia, interchanges of Greek φ and ου/υ in nonnative names likely reflects a fricative φ already by the Roman period: e.g., οαφα vs. ουαουα vs. ουαυα.[43] It is only in Egypt

41. Allen, *Vox Graeca*, 21.
42. Threatte, *Grammar of Attic Inscriptions I*, 347, 469–70.
43. Brixhe, *Grec anatolien*, 43; Brixhe, "Asia Minor," 235.

and Arabia (and the provincial dialects to the east generally) that we find a plosive φ = [pʰ] maintained throughout the Roman period,[44] which (at least in the case of the latter) may be the result of language contact, since contemporary Arabic likely had only [pʰ] but no [f].[45]

4.1.6 ϑ (PNTG §7.2.3)

Pedagogically, the consonant θ should be pronounced like the *th* sound in *bath*. This is called a voiceless interdental fricative (IPA /θ/).

θεός	/θεós/	[θεˈɔs]
ἦλθεν	/élθen/	[ˈelθen]
μαθητής	/maθetés/	[maθeˈtes]

Historically,[46] the consonant θ was probably still pronounced as an aspirated *t* sound in the first century, much like the pronunciation of English *t* in the word *tack*. This is called an aspirated voiceless alveolar stop (IPA /tʰ/).

θεός	/tʰεós/	[tʰεˈɔs]
ἦλθεν	/éltʰen/	[ˈeltʰen]
μαθητής	/matʰetés/	[matʰeˈtes]

In the Judeo-Palestinian material, there are several pieces of evidence from the late Roman or early Byzantine period that indicate a fricative [θ] realization: κοχχαθιων (for κοχαδιων) (*CIIP* 2179, 3rd–6th c. CE); ζειον (for θεῖον) (HAMM0049, 438–455 CE); χαιαμηθ (for καϊάμης) (ZOOR0214, 465 CE), (see *PNTG* §§7.1.3.1.II; 7.2.3.1.I; 7.7.1.1.I). At an earlier period, it is

---

44. Gignac, *Grammar of the Greek Papyri I*, 86–101; Ahmad Al-Jallad, "Graeco-Arabica I: The Southern Levant," in *Arabic in Context*, ed. Ahmad Al-Jallad (Leiden: Brill, 2017), 125–26.

45. Al-Jallad, "Graeco-Arabica I," 125–26.

46. See footnote 33.

probable that θ was still pronounced as an aspirated stop [tʰ]. There is no explicit evidence for a fricative θ in Judeo-Palestinian Greek earlier than the third century CE.

θ around the Mediterranean

At the time of the New Testament, there were likely at least some speakers in Asia Minor who pronounced θ as a fricative [θ]. In many (or most) other regional varieties, however, the aspirated stop [tʰ] was the dominant pronunciation. Although there is some very early (5th c. BCE) evidence for a fricative θ in Laconia, this may be disconnected from the more widespread change during the Koine period.[47] The earliest[48] evidence for the fricativization of θ in more General Koine is found in second- or third-century CE Anatolian spellings like φιλοτειμηθαμενος (for φιλοτιμησάμενος).[49] In the Jewish catacombs of Rome, on the other hand, which are dated to roughly the same period, θ appears to have maintained its stop pronunciation, even though φ had already become a fricative in the same dialect.[50] While the evidence from Attic inscriptions of the Roman period is ambiguous (or mixed),[51] Egypt and Arabia both appear to reflect the maintenance of a plosive θ well into the Byzantine period.[52] In the case of Egypt, this is likely due to language contact, since [θ] was lacking in the consonantal inventory

---

47. There is some evidence for θ = /tʰ/ → /θ/ in Laconian as early as the fifth century BCE (e.g., inscriptional σιος 'god; goddess'), but this should be regarded as distinct from the θ = /tʰ/ → /θ/ development in General Koine, since some of these dialects appear to have progressed this development all the way to θ = /s/. See Geoffrey Horrocks, *Greek: A History of the Language and Its Speakers* (Oxford: Wiley-Blackwell, 2014), 170.

48. Allen suggests that θ might have become a fricative around the same time as φ (ca. 1st/2nd c. CE) in light of the Pompeian spelling *lasfe* (for λασφη (← λάσθη)), but this example is questionable. For more, see Allen, *Vox Graeca*, 21–22.

49. Brixhe, *Grec anatolien*, 39, 57–58; Brixhe, "Asia Minor," 234–35.

50. Leon, "Jewish Catacombs," 226–29; Allen, *Vox Graeca*, 22.

51. Threatte, *Grammar of Attic Inscriptions I*, 469–70.

52. Gignac, *Grammar of the Greek Papyri I*, 86–101; Al-Jallad, "Graeco-Arabica I," 114–17.

of Coptic.[53] In the case of Arabia, it is possible that the provincial dialects farther to the east maintained a more conservative pronunciation.[54]

4.1.7 ʽ Rough Breathing (Spiritus Asper) (PNTG *§7.3.1*)

Generally, the historical *h* sound, represented by ʽ (rough breathing or *spiritus asper*) in modern texts, was not pronounced in Koine Greek at the time of the New Testament.

ὁ λόγος	/o lóγos/	[o̞ ˈlo̞γo̞s]
αἱ γραφαί	/ε γραφέ/	[ε γραˈφε]
ᾅδης	/áðes/	[ˈaðe̞s]

Some speakers (or registers), however, likely maintained this *h* sound. As such, it should be considered an optional pronunciation that is also valid for a first-century CE reconstruction. If pronounced, it is pronounced as a voiceless glottal fricative (IPA /h/).

ὁ λόγος	/ho lóγos/	[ho̞ ˈlo̞γo̞s]
αἱ γραφαί	/hε γραφέ/	[hε γραˈφε]
ᾅδης	/háðes/	[ˈhaðe̞s]

In the Judeo-Palestinian Greek material, aspiration confusion in prepositions preceding words beginning with *spiritus asper* is attested already from the first century CE: αφ α[ρ]χης (for ἀπ᾽ ἀ[ρ]χῆς), ε]φ εθνος (for ἐ]π᾽ ἔθνος), απ ημ[ερων (for ἀφ᾽ ἡμ[ερῶν) (8HevXIIgr, 50 BCE–50 CE); μετ ημων (for μεθ᾽ ἡμῶν) (5/6Hev5, 110 CE); καθ ετος (for κατ᾽ ἔτος) (5/6Hev16, 127 CE; XHev/Se64, 129 CE). This likely indicates that rough breathing (i.e., the sound /h/) had fallen out of the language

---

53. W. Sidney Allen, *Ancient Egyptian Phonology* (Cambridge: Cambridge University Press, 2020), 6.

54. Al-Jallad, "Graeco-Arabica I," 114–17.

(see *PNTG* §7.3.1.1). On the other hand, *spiritus asper* in Greek loanwords
in Hebrew exhibits variation, sometimes being represented by *he* ה (ʜ)
and sometimes being represented by *aleph* א (ʔ): e.g., ἡγεμών → הֵיגְמוֹן
(heymon) and ὑποθήκη → אֲפוֹתִיקִי (ʔappoθiqi). There is even one case
in which word-medial (etymological) /h/ is preserved in a Greek loanword in Hebrew: συνέδριον (from σύν + ἕδρα) → סַנְהֶדְרִין (senheðrin) (see
PNTG §7.3.1.2). This could indicate that some speakers in first-century
CE Judea-Palestine continued to pronounce /h/ while others did not,
though the precise dates at which these loanwords first entered Hebrew
is an important question.

ˈ around the Mediterranean

At the time of the New Testament, speakers who no longer pronounced
spiritus asper (i.e., the /h/ sound) likely coexisted alongside those who preserved it. Whether such variation was merely dialectal or had to do with
register remains an open question. The loss of *spiritus asper* (/h/) likely began in some pockets during the Hellenistic period but did not become universal until late in the Roman period. In Egypt, the loss of word-initial /h/
appears to have begun at least among a segment of the population already
in the Hellenistic period.[55] Although the evidence from Attic inscriptions
is not supremely clear, it would be reasonable to suppose that /h/ was lost
by some speakers in the Hellenistic or Roman period.[56] In the Jewish catacombs of Rome, despite some evidence that /h/ might have been retained
by some, it seems to have been lost in the speech of most.[57] Generally in
Koine, it may be said that the maintenance of appropriate aspiration in
phrases like καθ᾽ ἕκαστον continues until the second century CE.[58]

---

55. Gignac, *Grammar of the Greek Papyri I*, 133–38; Teodorsson, *Ptolemaic Koine*,
239–40.

56. Threatte, *Grammar of Attic Inscriptions I*, 504–6.

57. Leon, "Jewish Catacombs," 230–31.

58. Allen, *Vox Graeca*, 50–53.

4.1.8 κ (PNTG §7.4.1)

Generally, the consonant κ is pronounced similarly to English *k* (or a hard *c*) but without aspiration. Aspiration simply refers to the puff of air that comes out while you are making the sound of the consonant. In English, this is not a distinction we are used to making but it was very important in Greek. In the case of *k* (or *c*), note the different pronunciations when you say the words *kept* and *cool*. Hold your hand up in front of your mouth as you pronounce each of these and you will find that when you say *kept* you feel no (or little) puff of air but when you say *cool* you do feel a puff of air. This is the distinction—or at least at a distance on the spectrum thereof—between unaspirated *k* (IPA [k]; e.g., *kept* ['kɛpt]) and aspirated *k* (IPA [kʰ]; e.g., *cool* ['kʰul]). You should thus pronounce Koine Greek κ (*kappa*) as an unaspirated *k* (IPA /k/) like the *k* in *kept* for a first-century pronunciation. This is called an unaspirated voiceless velar stop (IPA /k/).

κόσμος	/kósmos/	[ˈkozmos]
νεκρός	/nɛkrós/	[nɛˈkros]
καλός	/kalós/	[kaˈlos]

Before front vowels, namely ι–ει, υ–οι, η–ηι (*η*), ε–αι, this unaspirated *k* sound is pronounced slightly more forward on the palate, similar to the pronunciation of *k* in the English word *key*, but still without aspiration. This "more-forward-on-the-palate" pronunciation of velar consonants like κ before front vowels is a phenomenon called *palatalization*. Although this phenomenon occurs with all the velar consonants (i.e., γ, κ, χ), it is simplest to explain the properties of palatalization here regarding the letter κ. Philemon Zachariou, a Greek linguist also invested in discussions regarding the pronunciation of Biblical Greek, explains as follows:[59]

> In pronouncing the made-up words *koo-kee, koo-kee*, you may notice a slight change between the *k* in *koo* and the *k* in *kee*. The change is due to the shift in tongue position from the back vowel *oo* [u] in *koo* to the front

---

59. Philemon Zachariou, *Reading and Pronouncing Biblical Greek: Historical Pronunciation Versus Erasmian* (Eugene, OR: Wipf & Stock, 2020), 120.

vowel *ee* [i] in *kee*. At *koo*, lips are rounded and the tongue is humped high up in the back of the mouth. As you proceed from *koo* to *kee*, lips spread and the tongue moves slightly forward against the hard palate. The change in tongue position from *koo*, in which the back of the tongue is against the velum, to *kee*, in which the front of the tongue moves against the palate, causes *velar k* to become *palatalized*. This type of palatalization is more noticeable in Greek.

This palatalized sound, then, which is an allophone of ϰ = /k/, is called an unaspirated voiceless palatal stop (IPA [c]). The ancient evidence raises some questions as to whether or not Koine Greek exhibited such palatalization before only [i] or before all the front vowels (i.e., [i], [y], [e], [ɛ]). In light of this ambiguity, it is recommended to follow the example of Neohellenic (Modern Greek), which exhibits palatalization before all the front vowels. There were likely some pronunciations of Koine Greek, however, that had palatalization before only [i] = ι–ει. You thus might also consider limiting your palatalization to such contexts.

κιβωτός	/kiβotós/	[ciβo̩'to̩s]
κεῖται	/kíte/	['cite]
κοινωνία	/kynonía/	[cyno̩'nia] (also: [kyno̩'nia])
κηρύσσω	/kerýso/	[ce'ruso̩] (also: [ke'ruso̩])
καί	/ke/	[ce] (also: [ke])

In the Judeo-Palestinian Greek material (as noted earlier), palatalization of velar consonants before front vowels is probably indicated by the inscriptional spelling ιη (for γῆ) attested at Beth She'arim (see §4.1.1). The fact that such palatalization is attested before the front vowel η, which had not yet merged with ι in Judeo-Palestinian Greek (see §4.3.3), likely indicates that velars were palatalized before all front vowels and not just before ι–ει = /i/.

ϰ(ι,υ,η,ε) around the Mediterranean

At the time of the New Testament, it was likely common for Koine Greek speakers to palatalize ϰ = [k] to [c] before front vowels. It is unlikely, however, that this feature was exhibited by all speakers or that palatalization occurred in precisely the same environments for those speakers who did exhibit it. Aside from parallel evidence connected with other velar consonants, such as γ, the primary evidence for ancient palatalization of ϰ comes from Coptic renderings of Greek words. In Coptic spellings of Greek words, a distinct palatal *k* symbol, also known as *cima* (Ϭ), is used before the front high vowel [i], but regular *k*, also known as *kab(b)a* (ⲕ), is used elsewhere. This is most clearly demonstrated in the Coptic rendering of the Greek word ϰαϰία = [ka'cia] as ⲕⲁϬⲓⲁ = [kakʲia], in which the first ϰ is represented by *kab(b)a* (ⲕ) and the second ϰ is represented by *cima* (Ϭ). It is significant that the palatal *cima* (Ϭ) is used before only the front high vowel [i], whereas *kab(b)a* (ⲕ) is used before all other vowels, including [e]. Such a usage is attested from around 350 CE.[60] This suggests that ϰ = [k] was palatalized to [c] before the vowel [i] (= ι, ει)—but not before η, υ, οι, ε, αι in Egyptian Koine. This is distinct from later/other forms of Greek, especially Neohellenic (Modern Greek), in which ϰ palatalizes to [c] before all front vowels: e.g., ϰῆπος = ['cipọs] and ϰαι = ['cẹ].[61]

After a nasal consonant, namely in the sequences (γ)ϰ or (ν)ϰ, the consonant ϰ undergoes voicing and is pronounced like *g* in the English word *dog*. As a result, the sequences γγ and γϰ are pronounced identically. This sound, which should be considered an allophone of ϰ = /k/, is called a voiced velar stop (IPA [g]).

ἀγϰάλαις	/ankáles/	[a(ŋ)'gales]
συνϰρῖναι	/synkríne/	[sy(ŋ)'grine]
ὄγϰος	/ónkos/	['ọ(ŋ)gọs]

Because the sequences γγ and γϰ are pronounced identically, this also means that, after a nasal consonant + before front vowels, (γ)ϰ is pronounced as a voiced palatal stop, which in turn brings about the palatalization of the preceding nasal.

60. Eduard Schweizer, *Griechische Grammatik: Erster Band: Allgemeiner Teil. Lautlehre. Wortbildung. Flexion* (München: Beck, 1939), 160; Bubenik, *Hellenistic and Roman Greece*, 264.

61. Holton, Mackridge, and Philippaki-Warburton, *Greek*, 5.

ἤνεγκεν   /énɛnkɛn/   [ˈɛnɛ(ɲ)ɟɛn]

ἄγκιστρον   /ánkistron/   [ˈa(ɲ)ɟi̥strọn]

ἀνάγκη   /anánke/   [aˈna(ɲ)ɟe]

There is no explicit evidence for the post-nasal voicing of χ in Judeo-Palestinian Koine, but this is probably due only to the limits of the corpus. It may be plausibly reconstructed, however, on the basis of the evidence for post-nasal voicing of π (see §4.1.9) and τ (see §4.1.10).

(γ)χ, (ν)χ around the Mediterranean

At the time of the New Testament, it is unclear how common it was for speakers to pronounce χ with voicing as [g] after nasal consonants. Explicit evidence for post-nasal voicing of χ may be found only in the Egyptian papyri, where interchanges between γχ ↔ γγ begin to crop up from the first century CE: e.g., αγκελλις (for ἀγγέλλεις) (P.Princ. 2.66, 1st c. CE) and ενγαλο (for ἐγκαλῶ) (Stud.Pal. 22.46, 2nd c. CE).[62] It is problematic, however, that the distinction between χ and γ was blurred for many speakers of Egyptian Koine due to bilingual interference.[63] In Anatolia, post-nasal voicing of χ in the Roman period was likely, but can be inferred from the data regarding only ντ (see §4.1.10).

In the preposition/prefix element ἐκ(-) before voiced consonants, namely β, γ, δ, ζ, λ, μ, ν, ρ, the consonant χ undergoes voicing and is pronounced like *g* in the English word *agnostic*.

ἐκ μέρους   /ɛk mérus/   [ɛgˈmɛru̥s]

ἐκ δεξιῶν   /ɛk ðeksión/   [ɛg ðɛˈksçọn]

ἐκδέχεσθαι   /ɛkðéxɛsθɛ/   [ɛgˈðɛxɛs̠θɛ]

In the Judeo-Palestinian material, scribes frequently spell "standard" ἐκ/ἐκ- before voiced consonants as εγ to indicate that χ was pronounced

---

62. Search via the TM Text Irregularities database. See Depauw and Stolk, "Linguistic Variation." See also Bubenik, *Hellenistic and Roman Greece*, 220.

63. Gignac, *Grammar of the Greek Papyri I*, 76–80.

with voicing in such environments: e.g., εγ βασιλεως (for ἐκ βασιλέως) (*CIIP* 3513, 217–204 BCE); εγβαλει (for ἐκβαλεῖν) (*CIIP* 3690, 2nd/1st c. BCE); εγνηψον (for ἔκνηψον) (8HevXIIgr, 50 BCE–50 CE); εγδικησωμεν (for ἐκδικήσωμεν) (5/6Hev20, 130 CE) (see *PNTG* §7.4.1.2.I). In fact, during the Hellenistic and Roman periods, "standard" ἐκ/ἐκ- before voiced consonants is spelled as εγ roughly 75% of the time.

ἐκ/ἐκ- around the Mediterranean

At the time of the New Testament, it is probable that many (or most) speakers of the various regional varieties of the Koine pronounced ἐκ/ἐκ- as [εg]/[ε̣g] before voiced consonants. Such assimilation in voicing is well attested in the Koine period and earlier.[64] In Attic inscriptions, such assimilations—e.g., εγβολη (for ἐκβολή) and εγδοσις (for ἔκδοσις)—constitute the normal orthography of the Hellenistic period, even though they become less common in Roman times.[65] In Anatolia, voicing assimilation of εκ → εγ is also attested in inscriptions of the late Roman period.[66] In Egypt, voicing assimilation of εκ → εγ is common in the Hellenistic period and continues on into the Roman period, but it may have been only an orthographic relic at that stage, since voiced and voiceless stops were underdifferentiated phonemically due to language contact.[67]

4.1.9 π (PNTG §7.4.2)

Generally, the consonant π is pronounced similarly to English *p* but without aspiration (cf. §4.1.8). Note, for example, the different pronunciations when you say the words 'happy' and 'pool'. The word 'happy' has no puff of air and the word 'pool' has a puff of air. This is the distinction between unaspirated *p* (IPA [p]; e.g., 'happy' ['hæpi]) and as-

---

64. Allen, *Vox Graeca*, 15.

65. Threatte, *Grammar of Attic Inscriptions I*, 579–86.

66. Brixhe, *Grec anatolien*, 37–38.

67. Gignac, *Grammar of the Greek Papyri I*, 173–76; Teodorsson, *Ptolemaic Koine*, 241–43.

pirated *p* (IPA [pʰ]; e.g., 'pool' ['pʰul]).[68] You should thus pronounce Koine Greek π (*pi*) as an unaspirated *p* (IPA /p/) like the *p* in 'happy' for a first-century pronunciation. This is called an unaspirated voiceless bilabial stop (IPA /p/).

ποιεῖν	/pyín/	[py'in]
πνεῦμα	/pnéβma/	['pnɛβma]
ἀγάπη	/aɣápe/	[a'ɣape]

After a nasal consonant, namely in the sequences (μ)π or (ν)π, the consonant π undergoes voicing and is pronounced like *b* in the English word *boy*. This sound, which is an allophone of p = /p/, is called a voiced bilabial stop (IPA [b]).

ἔμπροσθεν	/énprosθen/	['ɛ(m)brọsθen]
συνπαρόντες	/synparóntɛs/	[sy(n)ba'rọ(n)dɛs]
τὴν πόλιν	/ten pólin/	[te(n) 'bọlin]

In the Judeo-Palestinian Greek material, post-nasal voicing of π is evidenced in the Byzantine-period spelling λαμβρο(τατω) (for λαμπρο(τάτῳ)) (P Ness 3 26, 570 CE). Whether this post-nasal voicing also applied to π in earlier periods can be inferred only by comparative evidence.

μπ, νπ around the Mediterranean

At the time of the New Testament, it is unclear how widespread post-nasal voicing of π was. In Attic inscriptions, we do find ανβλεατος (for Latin *Ampliātus*) in a second-century CE Roman-period inscription, but this interchange does not appear in a native Greek word.[69] In Egyptian Koine, there are some cases of μπ ↔ μβ in the Roman period: e.g., εμπηναι (for ἐμβῆναι) (P.Oxy. 295.6, ca. 35 CE); εμβροστεν (for ἔμπροσθεν) (P.Ryl.Gr. 2.174a, 2nd

---

68. See Andrew Martin and Sharon Peperkamp, "Speech Perception and Phonology," in *Phonological Interfaces*, ed. Marc van Oostendrop et al., vol. 4 of *The Blackwell Companion to Phonology* (Malden: Wiley-Blackwell, 2011), 2334–36.

69. Threatte, *Grammar of Attic Inscriptions I*, 434–37.

c. CE).[70] It is not clear, however, how widespread this phenomenon was or to what degree it may have been the result of bilingual interference. In Anatolia, post-nasal voicing of π in the Roman period was likely but can be inferred based on the data regarding only ντ (see §4.1.10).

4.1.10 τ (PNTG §7.4.3)

Generally, the consonant τ is pronounced similarly to English *t* but without aspiration (cf. §4.1.8). Note, for example, the different pronunciations when you say the words *stop* and *tool*. The word *stop* has no puff of air and the word *tool* has a puff of air. This is the difference between unaspirated *t* (IPA [t]; e.g., *stop* ['stɑp]) and aspirated *t* (IPA [tʰ]; e.g., *tool* ['tʰul]). You should thus pronounce Koine Greek τ (*taf*) as an unaspirated *t* (IPA /t/) like the *t* in *stop* for a first-century pronunciation. This is called an unaspirated voiceless alveolar stop (IPA /t/).

τοῦτο	/túto/	['tuto̯]
τέλος	/télos/	['tɛlo̯s]
αὐτός	/aφtós/	[a'φto̯s]

After a nasal consonant, namely in the sequence (ν)τ, the consonant τ undergoes voicing and is pronounced like English *d*. This sound, which is an allophone of t = /t/, is called a voiced alveolar stop (IPA [d]).

πάντα	/pánta/	['pa(n)da]
λέγοντες	/léyontɛs/	['lɛɣo̯(n)dɛs]
πέντε	/péntɛ/	['pɛ(n)dɛ]

In the Judeo-Palestinian Greek material, there are two primary pieces of evidence that reflect post-nasal voicing of τ. In one late Byzantine inscription, post-nasal voicing of τ is unambiguously indicated by the spelling

---

70. Search via the TM Text Irregularities database. See Depauw and Stolk, "Linguistic Variation." See also Gignac, *Grammar of the Greek Papyri I*, 76–80.

φανενδος (for φανέντος) (*CIIP* Ap.18, 6th c. CE or later) (*PNTG* §7.4.3.2.I). That such post-nasal voicing was already present in the first century may be suggested by the following inscriptional spelling from Jerusalem: ιερον τρυφακτου (for ἱερὸν δρυφάκτου) (*CIIP* 2, 23 BCE–70 CE) (*PNTG* §7.1.3.2.I). Another piece of evidence in favor of early post-nasal voicing of τ comes in the form of the Greek word κοντός being rendered (as a loanword) in Mishnaic Hebrew as קוּנְדּוֹס (qunðos) (*PNTG* §7.4.3.5.III).

ντ around the Mediterranean

At the time of the New Testament, there is evidence that at least some speakers of Koine Greek were pronouncing τ with voicing as [d] after the nasal ν. It remains unclear, however, how widespread this phenomenon was. Post-nasal voicing of τ may have occurred generally in Koine by the Roman period, but the evidence for this phenomenon is not attested equally in different regional varieties. Moreover, because evidence for post-nasal voicing of κ and π is at best meager, most scholars have reconstructed post-nasal voicing of κ, π, τ based on the interchange ντ ↔ νδ, which is far more common. In Anatolia, this development is especially pronounced, so that we regularly find forms like αδιγονη (for ἀντιγόνη) and αντρι (for ἀνδρί) in Roman-period inscriptions. In fact, post-nasal voicing of τ is already attested in the fourth century BCE in Pamphylia in forms like πεδε (for πέντε) and γενοδαι (for γένωνται). It continues to be attested at a later date, as in first-century BCE spellings like δεκαπενδε (for δεκαπέντε).[71] In Attic inscriptions, although there is some variation of ντ ↔ νδ in some ethnic nouns, there are not actually any examples of such interchanges in native Greek words.[72] In Egypt, the tendency to voice post-nasal τ was weak during the Hellenistic period.[73] While we do find examples like αντρος (for ἀνδρός) attested at a significant rate in the Roman period, the merger of /d/, /t/ → /t/ under the influence of Coptic has resulted in τ ↔ δ interchanges being common in a variety of phonological environments.[74]

---

71. Brixhe, *Grec anatolien*, 34–37; Brixhe, "Asia Minor," 234; Bubenik, *Hellenistic and Roman Greece*, 239.

72. Threatte, *Grammar of Attic Inscriptions I*, 566–67.

73. Bubenik, *Hellenistic and Roman Greece*, 220.

74. Gignac, *Grammar of the Greek Papyri I*, 80–83.

4.1.11 μ (PNTG §7.5.1)

Generally, the consonant μ is pronounced like English *m*, namely as a voiced bilabial nasal (IPA /m/).

μόνος	/mónos/	['mǫnǫs]
ἡμῶν	/emón/	[e'mǫn]
σημεῖον	/semíon/	[se̩'miǫn]

Before a stop consonant, namely in the sequences μ(β) and μ(π), the consonant μ is pronounced weakly. In the Koine period, there is evidence that this weakness could lead to one of three situations: (i) the μ dropping out entirely, (ii) the μ dropping out and leaving behind a trace so that the vowel before the μ was pronounced with nasality, or (iii) the μ assimilating to the following β or π and making them double consonants (i.e., held for about 1.2x–2.5x longer duration). Any of these three realizations would be acceptable for a first-century CE pronunciation. It is plausible, however, that the dropping out of μ and nasalization of the preceding vowel was the most common. Nasalization of vowels is signified in the IPA by the ˜ sign: e.g., ã, ẽ, ĩ. In careful reading and slow speech, however, it is likely that speakers maintained the μ in these environments. In any case, in order to signify the weakness generally without obligating a particular pronunciation, [m] may be enclosed by parentheses before [b].

πέμπω	/pémpo/	['pɛ(m)bǫ] (prob. ['pɛ̃bǫ])
λαμβάνω	/lamβáno/	[la(m)'banǫ] (prob. [lã'banǫ])
συμβαίνει	/synbéni/	[sy(m)'bɛni] (prob. [sỹ'bɛni])

In the Judeo-Palestinian Greek material, the weakening of pre-stop μ is indicated explicitly by Byzantine spellings like λαπαδιου (for λαμπαδίου) (*CIIP* 896, 5th c. CE), σεβ[ι]ο(υ) (for συμβ[ί]ο(υ)) (HAMM0038, 4th–6th c. CE), and εσεφονησεν (for ἐσυμφώνησεν) (P Ness 3 56, 687 CE) (*PNTG* §7.5.1.1.IV–VI). A spelling like σαμβατου (for σαββάτου) (ZOOR0131, 427

CE) likely also reflects the tendency for μ to weaken and assimilate to the following stop (*PNTG* §7.1.2.2.I). That this phenomenon was already part of the language at an earlier stage, however, may be evidenced by the omission of a nasal consonant in the rendering of Greek loanwords in Hebrew: e.g., ἐμβατή → אבטה (ʔBTH) and κράμβη → כְּרוּב (kruv) (*PNTG* §7.5.1.4.III). The comparative material regarding pre-stop ν (see §4.1.12) also supports positing a relatively early date for this development.

μβ, μπ, μφ, etc. around the Mediterranean

At the time of the New Testament, in most regional varieties of the Koine, speakers tended to pronounce pre-stop μ more weakly. The weakening of pre-stop μ appears to have arisen at different times in different regional varieties of the Koine. In Attic inscriptions, beginning already in the fifth and fourth centuries BCE, μ is often omitted in pre-stop position, which reflects weakening: e.g., ολυπικος (for ὀλυμπικός).[75] In Egypt, weakening of μ before stops appears to be attested already in Hellenistic times. In some cases, this can lead to complete assimilation to the following stop and resulting gemination: e.g., μεταλαββανων (for μεταλαμβάνων) (P.Oslo. 3.153, 100–125 CE).[76] In Anatolian Koine, pre-stop μ can also be omitted from the orthography or assimilated (e.g., συββιον for σύμβιον), but these examples tend to be a bit later than those of Egypt and Attica.[77] In Italy, omission and/or assimilation of pre-stop μ is attested in the second- and third-century CE inscriptions of the Jewish catacombs of Rome.[78]

---

75. Threatte, *Grammar of Attic Inscriptions I*, 485–88.

76. Teodorsson, *Ptolemaic Koine*, 247–48; Bubenik, *Hellenistic and Roman Greece*, 239–40. Search also via the TM Text Irregularities database. See Depauw and Stolk, "Linguistic Variation."

77. Brixhe, *Grec anatolien*, 33–37; Bubenik, *Hellenistic and Roman Greece*, 239–40.

78. Leon, "Jewish Catacombs," 229–30.

4.1.12 ν (PNTG §7.5.2–3)

Generally, the consonant ν is pronounced like English *n*, namely as a voiced alveolar nasal (IPA /n/).

νόμος	/nómos/	[ˈnomọs]
ἐγένετο	/eɣéneto/	[εˈjenetọ]
νίπτομαι	/níptome/	[ˈniptọme]

Before a stop consonant, namely in the sequences ν(γ), ν(κ), ν(β), ν(π), ν(δ), ν(τ), the consonant ν is pronounced weakly. In the Koine period, there is evidence that this weakness could lead to one of three situations: (i) the ν dropping out entirely, (ii) the ν dropping out and leaving behind a trace so that the vowel before the ν would be pronounced with nasality, or (iii) the ν assimilating to the following stop and making it a double consonant (i.e., held for about 1.2x–2.5x longer duration). Any of these three realizations would be acceptable for a first-century CE pronunciation. One might favor the dropping out of ν and nasalization of the preceding vowel (e.g., ã) as the most common. In careful reading and slow speech, however, it is likely that speakers maintained the ν in these environments. In order to signify the weakness generally without obligating a particular pronunciation, [n] should be enclosed by parentheses before stops.

ἐνκακεῖν	/ɛnkakín/	[ε(ŋ)gaˈcin] (prob. [ε̃gaˈcin])
συνπορεύομαι	/synporéβome/	[sy(n)bọˈreβọme] (prob. [sỹbọˈreβọme])
ἄνδρα	/ándra/	[ˈa(n)dra] (prob. [ˈãdra])

In word-final position, especially when followed by a word beginning with a (stop) consonant, the consonant ν is pronounced weakly. Like the preceding example, the weakening of ν in such environments can result in (i) ν dropping out entirely, (ii) ν dropping out and leaving behind a nasalized vowel, or (iii) ν assimilating to the following consonant. Even though this phenomenon could happen with word-final ν in general, it was most common when the following word began with a consonant, and, in particular, a stop consonant. And, once again, this was probably avoided in careful reading. As such, it is not a necessary feature of first-century pronunciation. Nevertheless, if one wants to implement it, it is recommended to do so only when the following word begins with a consonant, particularly in the case of stops. This may be indicated by enclosing the ν in parentheses in such environments.

τὸν δοῦλον	/ton ðúlon/	[tǫ(n) 'dulǫn]
		(prob. [tǫ̃ 'dulǫn])
ἐν τῇ πόλει	/ɛn té póli/	[ɛ(n) 'de 'pǫli]
		(prob. [ɛ̃ 'de 'pǫli])
παιδίον καὶ	/peðíon kɛ/	[pɛ'ðiǫ(ɲ) ɟɛ]
		(prob. [pɛ'ðiǫ̃ ɟɛ])

In the Judeo-Palestinian Greek material, weakening of pre-stop ν is evidenced in spellings like εξωκιζωτον (for ἐξοικιζόντων) (*CIIP* 440, 1st c. BCE/CE) and ατιγονα (for ἀντιγόνα) (*CIIP* 513, 1st c. BCE/CE) (*PNTG* §7.5.2.1.III). Weakening of word-final ν is evidenced in spellings like λειτρο (for λίτρον) (Mas817, 19 BCE), εριο (for ἔριον) (*CIIP* 673, 1st c. CE), and ε τη αυτη αυλη (for ἐν τῇ αὐτῇ αὐλῇ) (5/6Hev20, 130 CE) (*PNTG* §7.5.2.1.II). Omission of word-final ν often occurs when the following word begins with a stop, but this is not always the case.

ντ, νβ, νπ, ν#, etc. around the Mediterranean

At the time of the New Testament, it is likely the case that many (or even most) speakers of Koine Greek pronounced ν weakly before a stop or in word-final position. Whether this resulted in complete omission (but with voicing of the following stop), assimilation to the following stop, or nasalization of the preceding vowel probably varied from speaker to speaker. Although this weakening is widely attested by the Roman period, the weakening of word-final and pre-stop ν does not appear to have arisen in each regional variety of the Koine at the same time. In Attic inscriptions, beginning already in the fifth and fourth centuries BCE, nasals are omitted in pre-stop position, which reflects weakening: e.g., πετε (for πέντε).[79] In Egypt, such nasal weakening is already attested from the end of the fourth century BCE. In some cases, this can lead to complete assimilation to the following stop and resulting gemination: e.g., προσηνεκκεν (for προσήνεγκεν) (P.Cair.Zen. 3.59443, 263–229 BCE).[80] In Anatolian Koine, most examples are dated significantly later than the earliest Attic and Egyptian examples, which suggests that word-final/pre-stop nasals were maintained longer there. This coheres well with modern dialectology, since there are even some Greek dialects in modern-day Turkey that maintain word-final nasals.[81] In Italy, omission and/or assimilation of pre-stop ν is attested in the second- and third-century CE inscriptions of the Jewish catacombs of Rome.[82] This phenomenon eventually became so pervasive that historical final ν has completely dropped out of numerous morphological paradigms in Modern Greek: e.g., τον ουρανό (cf. Koine τὸν οὐρανόν); την κόρη (cf. Koine τὴν κόρην).[83]

4.1.13 λ (PNTG §7.6.1)

The consonant λ is pronounced like English *l*, namely as a voiced alveolar lateral approximant (IPA /l/).[84]

λόγος	/lógos/	[ˈlo̞ɣo̞s]
ἄλλος	/álos/	[ˈalo̞s]
φίλος	/fílos/	[ˈɸilo̞s]

79. Threatte, *Grammar of Attic Inscriptions I*, 485–88.

80. Teodorsson, *Ptolemaic Koine*, 247–48; Bubenik, *Hellenistic and Roman Greece*, 239–40. Search also via the TM Text Irregularities database. See Depauw and Stolk, "Linguistic Variation."

81. Brixhe, *Grec anatolien*, 33–37; Bubenik, *Hellenistic and Roman Greece*, 239–40.

82. Leon, "Jewish Catacombs," 229–30.

83. See Holton, Mackridge, and Philippaki-Warburton, *Greek*, 58, 66.

84. There is some evidence for the weakening of λ, but this does not need to be included in pronunciation (see *PNTG* §7.6.1.1).

4.1.14 ρ (PNTG §7.6.2)

The consonant ρ is pronounced differently than English *r*. It would probably be better compared to Spanish *r*, though it is not entirely clear if Koine Greek ρ was more similar to the flap/tap *r* in Spanish *caro* (IPA ['kaɾo]) or the trilled *r* in Spanish *carro* (IPA ['karo]). Its pronunciation likely varied among different speakers. Neohellenic (Modern Greek) ρ is more of a flap/tap *r*, but this does not necessarily mean that this was the case in ancient times, where it might have been more trilled.[85] In any case, Greek ρ should be pronounced with your tongue touching the ridge of the mouth behind your teeth (i.e., in the same place where your tongue touches when you pronounce λ) for a Roman-period pronunciation. The IPA symbol /r/ will be used to signify Koine Greek ρ in my transcriptions, but either an alveolar tap/flap (IPA /ɾ/) or an alveolar trill (IPA /r/) could theoretically be acceptable for a first-century pronunciation. It should also be noted that by the Roman period, there was no distinction between ῥ and ρ (at least among most speakers).[86]

ῥῆμα	/réma/	['rema]
οὐρανός	/uranós/	[ura'nọs]
πατήρ	/patér/	[pa'ter]

Some speakers (or registers), however, likely maintained a distinction between voiced ρ = [r] and voiceless ῥ = [r̥], which occurs in word-initial position, after ρ, and after an aspirated stop. To make this sound, simply pronounce /r/ as above but without vibrating the vocal cords. In English this occurs in words like *tray*.[87] It can also help to think of pronouncing an [h] sound immediately before the [r] to give it its voiceless quality. Although it may not have been a mainstream pronunciation, there is evidence that it was present in the first century and thus should be considered optional. If one does adopt this sound in their pronunci-

85. See E. B. Petrounias, "The Pronunciation of Classical Greek," in *A History of Ancient Greek: From the Beginnings to Late Antiquity*, ed. A.-F. Christidis (Cambridge: Cambridge University Press, 2007), 563–64.

86. There is some evidence for the weakening of ρ, but this does not need to be included in pronunciation (see *PNTG* §7.6.2.1).

87. Petrounias, "Pronunciation of Classical Greek," 564.

ation, however, they should maintain *spiritus asper* (see §4.1.7) as well. In IPA transcription, voiceless ρ is represented as [r̥] (for the trill) or [ɾ̥] (for the tap/flap) with a circlet below the letter.

ῥῆμα	/réma/	[ˈr̥ema]
παῤῥησίᾳ	/pa(r)resía/	[pɑ(r̥)r̥eˈsiɑ]
θρόνος	/tʰrónos/	[ˈtʰr̥onọs] (if θ = [tʰ])

In the Judeo-Palestinian Greek material, the preservation of a voiceless ρ is indicated by some renderings of ῥ in Greek loanwords in Rabbinic Hebrew and Aramaic: e.g., ῥοδοδάφνη הרדפני (HRDPNY); ῥωμαῖος רהומיא (RHWMYʔ); παῤῥησία פרהסיה (PRHSYH) (*PNTG* §7.6.2.3.III).

ρ around the Mediterranean

At the time of the New Testament, it is possible that some dialects and/ or more formal registers maintained the distinction between voiced [r] and voiceless [r̥].

4.1.15 σ (PNTG §7.7.1)

Generally, the consonant σ is pronounced similarly to English *s*, but not exactly the same. It is retracted a bit, so it actually falls somewhere on the spectrum between English *s* (IPA /s/) and English *sh* (IPA /ʃ/). This is indicated in IPA transcription by a horizontal line/diacritic under the letter: i.e., [s̠]. To pronounce this sound, begin with an English *s* sound and slowly start to transform it into an English *sh* sound. Do this several times. As you feel your tongue move back in your mouth, stop in between *s* and *sh* and that will give you a retracted *s*. This is called a voiceless alveolar retracted sibilant (IPA /s̠/).

σύ	/sý/	[ˈs̠y]
γένεσις	/yénεsis/	[ˈjενεs̠is̠]
αὐτός	/aɸtós/	[aˈɸtọs̠]

Before voiced consonants, namely β, γ, δ, ζ, λ, μ, ν, ρ, the consonant σ undergoes voicing and is pronounced similarly to English *z*, but with the same retraction noted above. This sound, which is an allophone of σ = /s̱/, is called a voiced alveolar retracted sibilant (IPA [ẕ]).

κόσμος	/kósmos/	['ko̱zmo̱s]
πρεσβύτερος	/presβýteros/	[pre'zβyte̱ro̱s]
προσδοκᾷ	/prosδoká/	[pro̱zd̠o̱'ka]

In the Judeo-Palestinian Greek material, the retracted nature of σ is likely indicated by cases in which Greek σ is rendered with Hebrew *shin* ש (/ʃ/) in Jewish script:[88] e.g., ἀθηναγόρας → אתנגרש (ʔtngrš) (*CIIP* 456, 1st c. BCE/CE); νόμος → נומש (nwmš) (*CIIP* 693, 1st c. CE) (*PNTG* §7.7.1.6.VI). The voiced allophone of Greek σ is evidenced by spellings in which σ interchanges with ζ before voiced consonants: e.g., αγοραζματος (for ἀγοράσματος) (5/6Hev22, 130 CE); αμφιαζμου (for ἀμφιασμοῦ) (5/6Hev27, 132 CE); σιζμω (for σεισμῷ) (ZOOR0022, 363 CE). The voiced allophone of σ is also demonstrated by Hebrew renderings of Greek loanwords in the Mishnah like προσβολή → פְּרוֹזְבּוֹל (prozvol) (*PNTG* §7.7.1.6.II).

σ around the Mediterranean

At the time of the New Testament, it is likely that Greek speakers around the Mediterranean pronounced σ as a retracted [s̱]. Crosslinguistically, languages that have the sibilant /s/ but not /ʃ/ tend to realize the former with a more retracted pronunciation. The precise realization of σ in various regional varieties of the Koine, however, likely exhibited variation due to language contact with local languages. The voiced allophone of [ẕ] before voiced consonants was the normal Greek pronunciation in the Classical period and the Koine period and continues to be so in Greek today. It is reflected in Attic spellings like ψηφιζμα (for ψήφισμα) and ζμυρνα (for σμύρνα).[89] In Anatolian Koine, it is attested in Roman spell-

---

88. For the interpretation of ש as /ʃ/ over /s/ in such instances, see the full discussion in *PNTG* §7.7.1.6.VI.

89. Threatte, *Grammar of Attic Inscriptions I*, 510.

ings like πρεζβυτερος (for πρεσβύτερος).[90] In the Egyptian papyri, interchanges reflecting the voiced allophone of σ are common: e.g., νομιζματος (for νομίσματος) (O.Strasb. 1.776, 2nd c. CE). However, interchanges of σ and ζ are also common in other environments, which suggests that some speakers had merged ζ, σ → σ due to bilingual interference: e.g., αζημος (for ἄσημος) (*BGU* 3.854, 44/45 CE).[91]

4.1.16 ζ (PNTG §7.7.2)

The consonant ζ is pronounced similarly to English *z*, but it is retracted just like its voiceless counterpart σ (see above in §4.1.15). To pronounce it, follow the instructions given above for σ but vibrate the vocal cords. This is called a voiced alveolar retracted sibilant (IPA /z̺/).

ζωή	/zoé/	[z̺oˈe]
ἔζησεν	/ézes̺en/	[ˈɛz̺es̺en]
ἐλπίζω	/elpízo/	[elˈpiz̺o]

In the Judeo-Palestinian Greek material, the letter ζ, which was pronounced as /zd/ in the Classical period, had come to be pronounced as a singleton [z̺] by Roman times. This singleton pronunciation is exemplified by spellings like αγοραζματος (for ἀγοράσματος) (5/6Hev22, 130 CE) and αμφιαζμου (for ἀμφιασμοῦ) (5/6Hev27, 132 CE), in which ζ substitutes for singleton σ before voiced consonants.

ζ around the Mediterranean

At the time of the New Testament, there were likely Greek speakers who pronounced ζ as [z̺z̺], but many (or most) realized it simply as [z̺]. The original /zd/ pronunciation of ζ is exhibited in early (i.e., 6th/5th c. BCE)

---

90. Brixhe, *Grec anatolien*, 45–46; Brixhe, "Asia Minor," 236.

91. Gignac, *Grammar of the Greek Papyri I*, 120–24. Search also via the TM Text Irregularities database. See Depauw and Stolk, "Linguistic Variation."

Attic spellings like ζδευς (for ζεύς). Spellings like βυζζαντιοι (for βυζάντιοι) and βυσζαντιος (for βυζάντιος) likely reflect simplification of ζ = /zd/ → /zz/ during Hellenistic times. The convention of writing σζ for inter-vocalic ζ becomes rare after the Hellenistic period, which suggests that ζ had simplified to [z̠] by Roman times. Spellings like [ε]ιργαζμενο[ν] (for εἰργασμένον) are also attested in Attic inscriptions.[92] In Anatolian Koine, the convention of σζ for ζ also gains prominence in the Hellenistic period but lingers into Roman times only as a sporadic relic. Roman spellings like πρεζβυτερος (for πρεσβύτερος) likely indicate the further simplification to [z̠].[93] In the Jewish catacombs of Rome (ca. 2nd/3rd c. CE), interchanges like ζαβιου (for διὰ βίου), ζωναθα (for Hebrew /joːnaːθaːn/), and προζεκτω (for Latin *projecto*) may indicate that ζ was pronounced as an affricate [dʒ] or simple [z̠].[94] If the affricate sound is an accurate reconstruction, this may imply that the Italian variety of Koine originally had ζ = [dz].[95] On the other hand, the second-century CE grammarian Velius Longus seems to imply that ζ was pronounced as [z̠z̠] as late as the second century CE.[96] There were likely some differences of register with respect to the pronunciation of ζ. In Egypt, there is evidence that ζ = [z̠z̠] began to simplify to [z̠] early in the Hellenistic period.[97] An early simplification of ζ is likely connected to the early date for the general simplification of gemination in Egyptian Koine.[98]

4.1.17 ψ (PNTG §7.8.1)

The letter ψ is pronounced like the combination of π and σ, similar to English *ps* in the word *lapse*. It is not actually a phoneme in itself, but is made up of two separate phonemes, the unaspirated voiceless bilabial stop (IPA /p/) and the voiceless retracted alveolar sibilant (IPA /s̠/). As

92. Threatte, *Grammar of Attic Inscriptions I*, 546–49.
93. Brixhe, *Grec anatolien*, 45–46; Brixhe, "Asia Minor," 236.
94. Leon, "Jewish Catacombs," 230. See also Sturtevant, *Pronunciation*, 190.
95. Sturtevant, *Pronunciation*, 115.
96. Sturtevant, *Pronunciation*, 116–17. I would like to thank Luke Ranieri and Raphael Turrigiano for drawing my attention to this.
97. Teodorsson, *Ptolemaic Koine*, 190–91; Horrocks, *Greek*, 171.
98. Horrocks, *Greek*, 171.

such, the post-nasal voicing of /p/ (see §4.1.9) can also apply here (on a phonetic level).

ψυχή	/psyxé/	[psy'xe]
ἔγραψα	/éɣrapsa/	['ɛɣrapsa]
θλίψις	/θlípsis/	['θlipsis]
ἔπεμψα	/épempsa/	['ɛpɛ(m)bsa]

4.1.18 ξ (PNTG §7.8.2)

The letter ξ is pronounced like the combination of κ and σ, similar to English *cs* in the word *academics*. It is not actually a phoneme in itself, but is made up of two separate phonemes, the unaspirated voiceless velar stop (IPA /k/) and the voiceless retracted alveolar sibilant (IPA /s̠/). As such, the post-nasal voicing of /k/ (see §4.1.8) can also apply here (on a phonetic level).

ξύλον	/ksýlon/	['ksylon]
δόξα	/ðóksa/	['ðoksa]
σάρξ	/sárks/	['sarks]
ἔλεγξον	/élenkson/	['ɛlɛ(ŋ)gson]

4.1.19 Consonant Gemination (PNTG §7.9)

The concept of consonant gemination or "double consonants" is not necessarily familiar to most English speakers. To pronounce a consonant with gemination basically means to hold it for a duration roughly 1.2x–2.5x longer than its normal duration. For example, if you normally hold a consonant sound for 100 milliseconds, the geminated version of that consonant might be held for around 150 milliseconds. While gemination is part of the history of Greek—some dialects (e.g., Cypriot) even maintain it to this day—it had become neutralized in many dialects of the Koine, including Judeo-Palestinian, by the Roman period. As such, there should be no difference in pronunciation of double and single consonant letter sequences.

ἄλλος	/álos/	['alos̯]
θάλασσα	/θálasa/	['θalas̯a]
κρείττων	/kríton/	['kriton̯]

In the Judeo-Palestinian Greek material, the neutralization of phonemic gemination is indicated by frequent cases of CC → C: e.g., φιλιπιας (for φιλιππίας) (*CIIP* 2721, 1st c. BCE/CE); ιερισης (for ἱερίσσης) (*CIIP* 297, 1st c. BCE/CE); πιτακιου (for πιττακίου) (5/6Hev16, 127 CE); αλως (for ἄλλως) (5/6Hev52, 135 CE); εληνεστι (for ἑλληνιστί) (5/6Hev52, 135 CE) (see *PNTG* §7.9.2). Though less common, the hypercorrective reverse interchange C → CC also occurs: e.g., αππαν[τα (for ἅπαν[τα) (XHev/Se64, 129 CE) (see *PNTG* §7.9.3). From a chronological perspective, CC → C is attested roughly 4% of the time in the Hellenistic period, 11% of the time in the Roman period, and 18% of the time in the Byzantine period. This suggests that phonemic gemination began to be simplified in Hellenistic times and became progressively more widespread over time. While many speakers of the Roman period had neutralized phonemic gemination, there were likely some speakers and/or registers that maintained phonemic gemination of consonants in the first century.

CC around the Mediterranean

At the time of the New Testament, many speakers of Koine Greek around the Mediterranean no longer pronounced gemination in their everday speech. In certain dialects and/or in certain registers, however, phonemic gemination of consonants was maintained. The evidence for the simplification of consonant gemination varies widely based on the particular regional variety of the Koine. In the Egyptian material, for example, interchanges like αλοις (for ἄλλοις) are already common in the third century BCE, which suggests that the simplification of gemination began rather early in the Hellenistic period.[99] In Attic inscriptions, certain sequences, such as λλ or σσ (mostly in ethnic adjectives), seem to have been simplified by some segments of the population as early as the Hellenistic peri-

---

99. Gignac, *Grammar of the Greek Papyri I*, 154–65; Teodorsson, *Ptolemaic Koine*, 244–45.

od.[100] The interchange CC → C becomes more common toward the end of the Hellenistic period and into the Roman period.[101] In Anatolia, the simplification of geminate consonants also appears to go back to the Hellenistic period.[102] In Italy, singleton writings of λλ → λ, μμ → μ, νν → ν, ρρ → ρ, and σσ → σ in the Jewish catacombs of Rome would suggest the lack of gemination in the Roman period, but there are not enough data to be certain.[103] A more conservative pronunciation system and/or more formal/poetic register likely preserved gemination for longer than the colloquial register in each of these regional varieties. Philostratus's statement about a second-century CE Cappadocian rhetorician stumbling over consonants and syllable lengths might hint at such a reality.[104]

4.2 DIPHTHONGS

4.2.1 αυ, ευ, and ηυ (PNTG §§8.1.4–5; 8.2.4–5)

Generally (i.e., before vowels and voiced consonants), the final υ element of the diphthongs (α)υ, (ε)υ, and (η)υ is pronounced just like the normal pronunciation of β (see above in §4.1.2), namely as a "soft" *b* sound in between that of English *b* and *v*. Like the Spanish *b* and *v* sounds in words like *sabes* ['saβes] 'you know' or *favor* [fa'βor] 'favor', this sound is made with the lips together as if one were going to pronounce English *b* but by letting the airflow continue. This is called a voiced bilabial fricative (IPA /β/). Phonemically, it should probably be regarded as having merged with the phoneme β = /β/.

αὐλή	/aβlé/	[a'βle]
εὐαγγέλιον	/eβanγélion/	[εβα(ɲ)'ɟeliọn]
ηὐδόκησεν	/eβðókesen/	[e'βðǫceṣen]

100. Threatte, *Grammar of Attic Inscriptions I*, 511–27.

101. Sven-Tage Teodorsson, *The Phonology of Attic in the Hellenistic Period* (Göteborg: Acta Universitatis Gothoburgensis, 1978), 52–54.

102. Brixhe, *Grec anatolien*, 31–33; Brixhe, "Asia Minor," 234.

103. Leon, "Jewish Catacombs," 231.

104. See §4.3.8.

In Modern Greek, the υ element in these contexts is pronounced as a voiced labiodental fricative like English *v* (IPA /v/). The subtle shift of /β/ to /v/ probably occurred during the Byzantine period. For those who find /β/ difficult, pronouncing /v/ is a reasonable substitute.

αὐλή	/avlí/	[aˈvli]
εὐαγγέλιον	/evankélion/	[ęvα(n)ˈięlięn]
ηὐδόκησεν	/ivðókisen/	[iˈvðǫcişęn]

Before voiceless consonants (and in word-final position), this υ element undergoes devoicing and comes to be pronounced just like the normal pronunciation of φ (see above in §4.1.5), namely as a "soft" *p* sound in between that of English *p* and *f*. This sound is made with the lips together as if one were going to pronounce English *p* but by letting the airflow continue. This is called a voiceless bilabial fricative (IPA /ɸ/). Phonemically, it should probably be regarded as having merged with the phoneme φ = /ɸ/.

αὐτός	/aɸtós/	[aˈɸtǫş]
εὐθέως	/eɸθéos/	[εˈɸθεǫş]
ηὐχόμην	/eɸxómen/	[eɸˈxǫmen]

In Modern Greek, the υ element in these contexts is pronounced as a voiceless labiodental fricative like English *f* (IPA /f/). The subtle shift of /ɸ/ to /f/ probably occurred during the Byzantine period. For those who find /ɸ/ difficult, pronouncing /f/ is a reasonable substitute.

αὐτός	/aftós/	[aˈftǫş]
εὐθέως	/efθéos/	[ęˈfθęǫş]
ηὐχόμην	/ifxómin/	[ifˈxǫmin]

In the Judeo-Palestinian Greek material, fricativization of the υ element of the diphthongs is first indicated in the spelling αυδοκωσου (for ἀβδοκώσου) (*CIIP* 3635, 2nd/1st c. BCE), in which αβ interchanges with αυ (*PNTG* §7.1.2.1.I). The voiceless counterpart is indicated by Byzantine spellings such as αναπαψος (for ἀναπαύσεως) (*CIIP* 3264, Byzantine)

and εφυμιας (for εὐφημίας) (*CIIP* 3977, Byzantine) (*PNTG* §§8.2.4.1.IV;
§8.2.5.1.IV). A fricative pronunciation of the υ element of the diphthongs
ευ and αυ is also likely reflected in expanded spellings such as ιερεους
(for ἱερεύς) (*CIIP* 2178, 3rd/4th c. CE) (*PNTG* §8.2.5.1.II) and αυουτης (for
αὐτῆς) (*CIIP* 1548, 3rd–6th c. CE) (*PNTG* §8.2.4.1.III). This interpretation
is supported by the fact that the Latin sequence *av* can be rendered
this way: e.g., φλαυουιου (for Latin *Flavius*) (5/6Hev21, 130 CE) (*PNTG*
§7.10.1.2.II).

The rendering of Greek names and loanwords into Hebrew and Aramaic during the Roman period also provides early evidence for the
fricativization of the second element of these diphthongs: e.g., λευκόν
→ לבקן (LBQN) (Mishnah); εὔτολμος → אפטלמוס (?PṬLMWS) (*CIIP* 407,
1st c. BCE/CE); εὔτολμος → אפתלמיס (?PTLMYS) (XHev/Se50, 75–135
CE) (see *PNTG* §8.2.5.4.I–II). Given the fact that Hebrew/Aramaic *bet*
ב (B) and *pe* פ (P) were realized as fricatives after vowels, these examples may be taken as evidence for the fricativization of the second element of the diphthongs (with voiced and voiceless variants) by the
Roman period.

αυ, ευ, etc. around the Mediterranean

At the time of the New Testament, it is probable that many Koine Greek
speakers were already pronouncing a diphthong like αυ as [αβ]/[αφ] or
[αβ(^{w})]/[αφ(^{w})]—note that in IPA conventions superscript ʷ indicates that
a consonant is pronounced with labialization (i.e., rounding of the lips). It
is likely, however, that a more conservative pronunciation of [aṷ] or [aw]
was maintained in some dialects and/or registers. In Attic inscriptions,
interchanges of ευφ → εφ, such as εφρονις (for εὐφρονίς) and εφραιος (for
εὐφραῖος), *may* indicate that the second element of the diphthong had
already become a consonantal [φ] or [f] by Hellenistic or Roman times.[105]
In Egypt, the second-century BCE spelling ραυδους (for ῥάβδους) (*UPZ* 1.12,
1.13, 2nd c. BCE) seems to reflect fricativization of the second element of
this diphthong, but this phenomenon may not have been widespread until

---

105. Threatte, *Grammar of Attic Inscriptions I*, 345–48.

the Roman period.[106] While αβ/εβ ↔ αυ/ευ interchanges are more common (than αφ/εφ ↔ αυ/ευ) at an earlier period, even before voiceless consonants, we do find the form αφτων (for αὐτῶν) (P.Amst. 1.48, 6th c. CE) in Byzantine times.[107] This may indicate that [β] was generally regarded as the "default" pronunciation of the second element of the diphthongs, perhaps because it occurred more frequently (i.e., pre-voiced consonants *and* pre-vocalic). In Anatolia, the second element of αυ/ευ had already come to be pronounced as a fricative by the time of our second-century CE attestations, as demonstrated by spellings like κατεσκεβασεν (for κατεσκεύασεν) and αναπαβετε (for ἀναπαύεται).[108] In Italy, it is probable that the second element of the diphthong had become consonantal by the time of our second-century CE attestations: e.g., γραμματεους (for γραμματεύς).[109]

4.2.2 υι (PNTG §8.2.3)

Generally, the diphthong υι, which mainly appears in the word υἱός 'son' and forms of the feminine perfect participle, is pronounced just like υ. As we will see below (see §4.3.2), υ is pronounced like the *ee* sound in English (e.g., in the word *meet*) but with accompanying rounding of the lips. This sound is called a front close rounded vowel (IPA /y/).

υἱός	/yós/	[yʼọs]
εἰδυῖα	/idýa/	[iˈðya]
ἐληλυθυῖα	/elelyθýa/	[ɛlelyˈθya]

106. Gignac, *Grammar of the Greek Papyri I*, 226–34; Teodorsson, *Ptolemaic Koine*, 229–31; Horrocks, *Greek*, 167–68. Search also via the TM Text Irregularities database. See Depauw and Stolk, "Linguistic Variation."

107. Search via the TM Text Irregularities database. See Depauw and Stolk, "Linguistic Variation."

108. Brixhe, *Grec anatolien*, 57–58; Brixhe, "Asia Minor," 233.

109. Leon suggests that ευ was still a true diphthong, but the interchanges ευ → εο, εου probably reflect the consonantalization (with rounding/labialization) of the second element of the diphthong: i.e., either [ɛw] or [ɛβ(ʷ)]/[ɛɸ(ʷ)]. See Leon "Jewish Catacombs," 224–25.

Some speakers (or registers), however, likely maintained the sequence υι as a true diphthong. As such, it should be considered an optional pronunciation that is also valid for a first-century CE reconstruction. The true diphthong, then, would be pronounced as a front close rounded vowel (IPA /y/)—*ee* with lip-rounding—followed by a front close unrounded vowel (IPA /i/)—*ee* without lip-rounding. To indicate the diphthongal nature, the second vowel is indicated with an inverted breve below (i.e., /yi̯/).

υἱός	/yi̯ós/	[yi̯'os]
εἰδυῖα	/iðýi̯a/	[i'ðyi̯a]
ἐληλυθυῖα	/elelyθýi̯a/	[elely'θyi̯a]

In the Judeo-Palestinian Greek material, most of the evidence suggests that υι was pronounced as a single /y/ vowel from the Roman period onward: e.g., υου (for υἱοί) (*CIIP* 451, 1st c. BCE/CE); υος (for υἱός) (*CIIP* 548, 1st c. BCE/CE); υο (for υἱοῦ) (5/6Hev15, 125 CE); υος (for υἱός) (BETH0094, 3rd c. CE); υος (for υἱός) (*CIIP* 1140, 5th–6th c. CE) (*PNTG* §8.2.3.1). There are, however, a collection of spellings that appear to reflect the preservation of the diphthong at a late period: e.g., οιιος (for υἱός) (*CIIP* 2178, 3rd–4th c. CE); υειοις (for υἱοῖς) (HAMM0002, 455 CE); υειου (for υἱοῦ) (*CIIP* 2243, 3rd–5th c. CE) (*PNTG* §8.2.3.2). This may indicate either that both pronunciations coexisted in earlier periods or that Byzantine scribes—and possibly users of the language—attempted to reinstitute the more "Attic" or "Classical" pronunciation of the diphthong at a later date.

υι around the Mediterranean

At the time of the New Testament, it is probably the case that in the everyday speech of many (or most) speakers, υι was pronounced identically to υ as a single /y/ vowel. This pronunciation, however, appears to have coexisted alongside a more conservative pronunciation that maintained the diphthong. In Attic inscriptions, pre-vocalic υι is pronounced simply as υ already from an early period, as evidenced by the universal spelling υος (for υἱός) in Hellenistic times. In the Roman period, however, the ι was restored (both orthographically and in pronunciation) so that υιος became the normal spelling by 50 CE; variants like υειος and υειοι are also attested in late Roman times.[110] In Egypt, there is some evidence for a minority monophthong pronunciation in the third century BCE, but otherwise the ι vowel seems to have been maintained. By the Roman period, this ι vowel may have even become a glide [j] in pre-vocalic position.[111] The Egyptian papyri also attest to the expanded spelling in the feminine participle: e.g., γεγονυειαι (for γεγονυῖαι) (*CPR* 15.3, 1st c. CE).[112] In Anatolia, a variety of spellings for words like υἱός (e.g., υιος, υος, υειος, ειου, ιου) indicate that the pronunciation of the diphthong υι as either [yi̯] or [y] was by no means consistent.[113] Italy, similarly, exhibits multiple spellings: υειος, υος, υω.[114]

4.3 Vowels

4.3.1 ι–ει (PNTG §8.3.1–4)

Generally, the vowel represented by ι–ει is pronounced like *ee* in English *meet*. This is called a front close unrounded vowel (IPA /i/).

ἰδού	/iðú/	[i'ðu]
λίθος	/líθos/	['liθo̞s]
πατρί	/patrí/	[pa'tri]
εἶπεν	/ípen/	['ipen]
πετεινόν	/petinón/	[peti'no̞n]
λέγει	/léɣi/	['lɛ̞ji]

110. Threatte, *Grammar of Attic Inscriptions I*, 338–44.

111. Gignac, *Grammar of the Greek Papyri I*, 202–8; Teodorsson, *Ptolemaic Koine*, 226–27.

112. Search via the TM Text Irregularities database. See Depauw and Stolk, "Linguistic Variation."

113. Brixhe, *Grec anatolien*, 48.

114. Leon, "Jewish Catacombs," 224.

In earlier stages of Greek, ει was pronounced like ι = [iː] generally but as [eː] before vowels. In the Judeo-Palestinian Greek material, the merger of ει, ι → ι in pre-vocalic position began during the Hellenistic period and was completed by Roman times: e.g., ανετειως (for ἀναιτίως) (*CIIP* 3689, 200–150 BCE); θρησκιας (for θρησκείας) (NAZARETH, 27 BCE–14 CE); φολεια (for Latin *Furia*) (*CIIP* 423, 1st c. BCE/CE); επαρχειας (for ἐπαρχίας) (5/6Hev5, 110 CE). There is plenty of evidence for the equivalence of ει and ι generally in the early Roman period: e.g., επιδιξη (for ἐπιδείξῃ) (NAZARETH, 27 BCE–14 CE); δ]εδανισμενοι (for δ]εδανεισμένοι) (XHev/Se66, 99–109 CE); επι (for ἐπεί) (5/6Hev30, 125 CE) (see *PNTG* §§8.3.1.1.I; 8.3.4.1.I).

At the same time, however, Roman-period scribes tend to substitute ει for etymologically long ῑ far more frequently than for etymologically short ῐ. This suggests that phonemic vowel length distinctions were still preserved in at least some more conservative pronunciation systems of the first century CE: e.g., αμετακεινητους (for ἀμετακῑνήτους) (NAZARETH, 27 BCE–14 CE); τειμαν (for τῑμᾶν) (NAZARETH, 27 BCE–14 CE); νεικη (for νίκη) (*CIIP* 2761, 2nd c. CE or earlier); μεικρου (for μῑκροῦ) (5/6Hev5, 110 CE) (for more, see *PNTG* §8.3.2.1.I).

Because the goal of this book is to present the reader with the more innovative "colloquial" pronunciation of the first century CE, the pronunciation recommended here is based on an isochronous system of vowels (i.e., no phonemic length distinctions in the vowel system). While this was likely the case for many speakers in first-century CE Judea-Palestine, the evidence from the ῑ → ει interchange demonstrates with little doubt that there were also many speakers who maintained a more conservative pronunciation with phonemic vowel length. There is some evidence that the more conservative pronunciation was associated with higher levels of education, formal registers, or both (see *PNTG* §§8.3.2.1.I; 9.2), but it is possible that the innovative and conservative pronunciations existed side-by-side apart from such sharp sociolinguistic divisions. It is not totally clear at what point the innovative isochronous system overtook the system with phonemic length distinctions as the *majority* pronunciation system, but it likely took place by the second century CE at the latest.

ει around the Mediterranean

At the time of the New Testament, most speakers of Koine Greek pronounced ει with the same vocalic quality as ι. Whether it was pronounced long as /iː/ or without length as /i/ depended on the preservation or neutralization of phonemic vowel length in the particular variety (and/or register) of the Koine (for more on this, see §4.3.8). Although it is common for introductory Greek textbooks to present ει as an e-vowel, it was actually already realized as [iː] from a very early period. In Attic inscriptions, the shift of ει = [eˑ] → [iˑ] (but not before vowels) began already in the fourth century BCE. Before vowels, however, the [eˑ] pronunciation of ει was preserved as an allophone, which likely persisted throughout Hellenistic times, as evidenced by spellings like αρηου (for ἀρείου) even as late as the first century CE. At the same time, the first century is also when we start to find interchanges like αριου (for ἀρείου), which show that ει had come to be pronounced like ι also before vowels for some speakers.[115] In Egypt, there is evidence that ει was pronounced with the same vocalic quality as ι (but not before vowels) already in the fourth century BCE. The subsequent change of pre-vocalic ει = [eː] → [iː] is probably attested among a minority of speakers at a relatively early stage, but there is in fact no evidence for a general shift of ει = [eː] → [i(ː)] until Roman times.[116] In Anatolia, the raising of non-pre-vocalic ει = [eː] to [iː] is attested in the third century BCE in Magnesia and in the second century BCE in Miletos. The subsequent raising of pre-vocalic ει = [eː] to [iː] is attested in Magnesia by the first century CE. By the time of our second-century CE attestations, ει and ι have completely merged.[117] In Italy, ει has completely merged with ι = /i/ by the time of our second-century CE attestations.[118]

In the sequence consonant + (unstressed) ι–ει + (non-/i/) vowel, the vowel represented by ι–ει *sometimes* undergoes palatalization and is

115. Threatte, *Grammar of Attic Inscriptions I*, 190–207.

116. Gignac, *Grammar of the Greek Papyri I*, 189–91; Teodorsson, *Ptolemaic Koine*, 212–15.

117. Brixhe, *Grec anatolien*, 46–49; Brixhe, "Asia Minor," 232–33; Bubenik, *Hellenistic and Roman Greece*, 245.

118. Leon, "Jewish Catacombs," 221–23.

pronounced like a "tight" *y* with continued airflow, that is, in the same way that γ is pronounced before front vowels (see §4.1.1). This sound, which is considered an allophone of ι–ει = /i/, is called a voiced palatal fricative (IPA [ʝ]). After voiceless consonants, this sound was likely pronounced without vibrating the vocal cords as a voiceless palatal fricative (IPA [ç]). Such a pronunciation was likely more colloquial, characteristic of fast speech, and thus unlikely to occur in slow and careful reading. As such, it should be regarded as an optional feature of pronunciation.[119]

δηνάριον	/ðenárion/	[ðeˈnarjon]
δαιμόνια	/ðemónia/	[ðɛˈmonja]
διαθήκη	/ðiaθéke/	[ðjaˈθece]
συμπόσια	/synpósia/	[sy(m)ˈbosça]
ἤσθιον	/ésθion/	[ˈesθçon]
ἱμάτια	/imátia/	[iˈmatça]

In the Judeo-Palestinian Greek material, there is some evidence that ι in these environments was realized as a palatal fricative. Especially after a sonorant (or κ) and before a back vowel, there is a tendency for ι to be omitted from the spelling: e.g., δ[η]ναρον (for δ[η]νάριον) (5/6Hev11, 124 CE); ημιωραν (for ἡμιωρίαν) (on a stressed syllable here) (XHev/Se64, 129 CE); πατρικος (for πατρίκιος) (*CIIP* 3735, 37 BCE–135 CE) (see *PNTG* §8.3.1.3). Such omission may indicate that it had become a sound not typically reflected in the script. This phenomenon also appears to be exhibited in Hebrew renderings of Greek loanwords in the Mishnah: e.g., στρατιά →אִסְרַטְיָיא (ʔisratya) and διαθήκη → דְּיָיתִיקֵי (dyaθiqe) (*PNTG* §8.3.1.6.V).

---

119. In some cases, this phenomenon can also occur with stressed /i/: e.g., κυρία /kyría/ [cyˈrja]. See Horrocks, *Greek*, 169. Palatalization of stressed /i/ in such environments need not be a regular feature of one's Koine Greek pronunciation but may be learned for a few select words: κυρία = [cyˈrja], δηναρίων = [ðenaˈrjon], etc. Palatalization of stressed /i/, however, is not recommended as a general rule for the Koine Greek pronunciation system outlined in this volume.

ια, ιω, ιου, etc. around the Mediterranean

At the time of the New Testament, it was not uncommon for speakers of Koine Greek to exhibit palatalization of ι before a back vowel. This appears to be attested in the Egyptian papyri: e.g., κυρου (for κυρίου) (P.Ryl. Gr. 2.160c, 32 CE); αργυρου (for ἀργυρίου) (P.Yale 1.63, 64 CE).[120] It may also be attested in Italy in spellings like ζαβιου (for διὰ βίου).[121]

At the beginning of a word before a non-/i/ vowel—this is merely a specific application of the preceding rule in another environment—the vowel represented by ι–ει (when unstressed) also undergoes palatalization and is pronounced as a voiced palatal fricative (IPA [j]). As above, this feature was possibly avoided in slow and careful reading and thus should be regarded as optional.

ἰατρός	/iatrós/	[jaˈtrǫs]
ἱερεύς	/ieréφs/	[jɛˈrɛφs]
εἰωθός	/ioθós/	[jǫˈθǫs]

In the Judeo-Palestinian Greek material, such a pronunciation may be indicated by the omission of word-initial ι in spellings like ησους (for ἰησοῦς) (5/6Hev15, 125 CE). Omission in this case may be due to the consonantal pronunciation of ι, though other explanations are possible.

#ια, #ιε, etc. around the Mediterranean

At the time of the New Testament, there is evidence that speakers in various regions were already pronouncing word-initial ι–ει /i/ with a palatalized allophone of [j] in some contexts. In Egypt, such a phenomenon may be exhibited by the addition of a superfluous γ in first-century BCE spellings like ιγερα (for ἱερά) (BGU 4.1197, 1st c. BCE).[122] In Anatolia, palatalization

---

120. Gignac, *Grammar of the Greek Papyri I*, 302–4.
121. Leon, "Jewish Catacombs," 230. See also Sturtevant, *Pronunciation*, 190.
122. Search via the TM Text Irregularities database. See Depauw and Stolk, "Linguistic Variation."

of word-initial ι–ει is indicated by Roman-period spellings like γατρος (for ἰατρός).[123] This even comes to be codified in certain Modern Greek spellings like γιατρός 'doctor' (cf. ancient Greek ἰατρός), though this orthographic phenomenon does not occur in all such environments.

Finally, when iota has diaeresis (i.e., ϊ), it is pronounced separately from the preceding vowel, so that αϊ = /ai/ but αι = /ε/ (see §4.3.4), ωϊ = /oi/ but ωι (ῳ) = /o/ (see §4.3.6), etc.

καϊάφας	/kaiáɸas/	[kaˈjaɸɑs]
στάχυϊ	/stáxyi/	[ˈstaçyi]
πρωϊνός	/proinós/	[prọiˈnọs]

In the Judeo-Palestinian Greek material, such a pronunciation can be indicated by the ϊ → ει (or even ϊ → ιει) interchange in spellings like ααβαει (for ἀαβαϊ) (Μur103, 100–135 CE) and τροπαιεικον (for τροπαϊκὸν) (5/6Hev 15, 125 CE). In some cases, the *diaeresis* is actually written in the ancient text: e.g., τραϊανου (for τραϊανοῦ) (Μur115, 124 CE).

ϊ **around the Mediterranean**

At the time of the New Testament, *iota* with *diaeresis* was consistently pronounced separately from the preceding vowel. Scribes would often indicate this explicitly in the orthography by substituting the digraph ει for ϊ. In Egyptian Koine, the strategy of marking αϊ with αει is attested in forms like τραειανου (for τραϊανοῦ) (P.Mich. 3.201, 99 CE). Forms like ρωμαεικην (for ῥωμαϊκήν) (P.Freib. 2.9, 138–161 CE) are attested in the Hellenistic period, and forms like γαειος (for γάϊος) (O.Berenike. 1.102, 33 CE; P.Mich. 2.127, 45–46 CE; P.Oslo. 2.33, 29–34 CE) and πτολεμαειχα (for πτολεμαϊχά) (O.Berenike. 1.101, 26–75 CE) are attested in first-century CE papyri. Forms like κοεινtου (for κοϊντου) (P.Oxy. 7.1023, 138–161 CE) and πλοεισμου (for πλοϊσμοῦ) (P.Vind.Tand 19, 426–475 CE) are attested in Roman and Byzan-

123. Brixhe, *Grec anatolien*, 39–40.

tine papyri, respectively.[124] In Attic Koine, we find both ï and ει being used in the same contexts: e.g., γαϊος and γαειος (for γάϊος); ζοειλος (for ζωῖλος).[125]

4.3.2 υ–οι (PNTG §§8.2.2; 8.3.5)

The vowel represented by υ–οι is pronounced like *ee* in English *meet* but with the lips rounded. This is called a front close rounded vowel (IPA /y/).

ὕδωρ	/ýðor/	['yðǫr]
βαρύς	/βarýs/	[βaˈrys̰]
λύομαι	/lýomε/	['lyǫmε]
οἶδα	/ýða/	['yða]
οἱ πολλοί	/y polý/	[y pǫˈly]
λοιπόν	/lypón/	[lyˈpǫn]

In Modern Greek (and perhaps in a very small minority of regional varieties during the Roman period), the vowel υ–οι had already merged with ι–ει and was pronounced as a front close unrounded vowel /i/. This is its pronunciation in Modern Greek. Unlike the case of η = /e/ or /i/, for which there was significant variation during the Roman period in different regional varieties of the Koine, the merger of υ–οι and ι–ει would have been much rarer. It seems not to have occurred universally in Greek until the end of the first millennium CE. Therefore, if one wanted to use a Modern Greek pronunciation of υ–οι = /i/, it could be justified historically in light of the small minority of regional varieties that had already generalized such a merger, but it would by no means have been the most common pronunciation heard around the Mediterranean during the Roman period.

---

124. Gignac, *Grammar of the Greek Papyri I*, 72. Search also via the TM Text Irregularities database. See Depauw and Stolk, "Linguistic Variation." Search also via Papyri.info.

125. Threatte, *Grammar of Attic Inscriptions I*, 200–201.

ὕδωρ	/íðor/	['iðǫr]
βαρύς	/varís/	[va'ris]
λύομαι	/líome/	['liǫmę]
οἶδα	/íða/	['iða]
οἱ πολλοί	/i polí/	[i pǫ'li]
λοιπόν	/lipón/	[li'pǫn]

In the Judeo-Palestinian Greek material, the merger of οι, υ → υ is demonstrated by spellings like the following: τυς (for τοῖς) (*CIIP* 452, 1st c. BCE/CE); ηνυγμενα (for ἠνοιγμένα) (5/6Hev20, 130 CE); ευμυρι (for εὐμοίρει) (BETH0002, 150–250 CE); ανυξε (for ἀνοῖξαι) (BETH0129, 3rd c. CE); κοινωνι (for κοινωνοί) (BETH0083, 200–350 CE); εμει (for ἐμοί) (BETH01012, 200–350 CE) (*PNTG* §8.2.2.1). Such interchanges begin in the first century but do not become especially common until the second and third centuries. This suggests that this merger had taken place among only a portion of the population—those with a more innovative "colloquial" register—in the first century but gradually came to be the majority pronunciation in the second and third centuries CE.

Alongside the first-century pronunciation of οι as /y/, then, there likely coexisted other pronunciations such as /ø̞/, /øy/, /øː/, and /ø/, all of which reflect intermediate stages in the merger. Note that the IPA vowel /ø/ is like the vowel /e/ but with lips rounded. Because this book presents the more innovative register of the first century—including those cases where developments begin among a portion of the population in the first century and do not become majority pronunciations until the second century—I recommend pronouncing οι as /y/.

Finally, it should also be noted that all the way through the Byzantine period, the οι → υ interchange is always significantly more common than the οι → ι interchange. This suggests that the merger of υ–οι, ι → ι was never more than a minority pronunciation in the Koine period. It was not until the medieval period that υ–οι merged with ι as in Modern Greek.

οι around the Mediterranean

At the time of the New Testament, the historical diphthong οι was likely in the process of becoming a monophthong and eventually merging with υ. As a result, one would probably encounter a variety of pronunciations around the Mediterranean. Some speakers likely still pronounced it as a diphthong like /ø̞/ (from earlier /o̞/) or perhaps even /øy/, while others probably monophthongized it to a long vowel /ø:/ or /y:/. Some more innovative pronunciation systems had already merged οι with υ in the first century. Whether οι = υ = /y/ was a minority or majority pronunciation in the first century, however, varied greatly depending on the region.

In Egypt, for example, there are already a significant number of οι → υ interchanges attested in the third and second centuries BCE: e.g., μυθυμεως (for μοιθύμεως) (P.Cair.Zen. 3.59407, 3rd c. BCE); ανυγω (for ἀνοίγω) (P.Lond. 7.2009, 3rd c. BCE); ανυξαι (for ἀνοῖξαι) (P.Köln.Gr. 8.342, 3rd c. BCE); τυχοι (for τοῖχοι) (P.Amh.Gr. 2.54 + P.Survey 55 descr., 2nd c. BCE); τυαυτην (for τοιαύτην) (P. L.Bat. 22.11, 2nd c. BCE).[126] This likely reflects monophthongization of οι (possibly to [ø(:)]) at this time, even if it did not completely merge with υ = /y/ until the early Roman period.[127] The early monophthongization of οι in Egypt may be related to the relatively early onset of isochrony there. In Attic inscriptions, on the other hand, the monophthongization of οι was actually quite late, not merging with υ until the late Roman period.[128] In Anatolia, οι had already merged with υ by the time of our second-century CE attestations. It is argued that υ itself had already iotacized, so that οι = υ = ι.[129] In Italy, the merger of οι and υ is reflected in our second-century CE attestations in Latin transcriptions such as *cymesis* (for κοίμησις).[130]

Finally, when upsilon has diaeresis (i.e., ϋ), it is pronounced separately from the preceding vowel, so that αϋ = /ay/ but αυ = /aβ, aφ/ (see §4.2.1), οϋ = /oy/ but ου = /u/ (see §4.3.7), etc.

126. Search via the TM Text Irregularities database. See Depauw and Stolk, "Linguistic Variation."

127. Gignac, *Grammar of the Greek Papyri I*, 197–202; Teodorsson, *Ptolemaic Koine*, 227–29; Horrocks, *Greek*, 165–69.

128. Threatte, *Grammar of Attic Inscriptions I*, 337.

129. Brixhe, *Grec anatolien*, 47–48; Brixhe, "Asia Minor," 232. The interchanges that Brixhe lists on p. 48, however, should raise suspicion that υ–οι may not yet have merged completely with ι.

130. Leon, "Jewish Catacombs," 224.

πραῢς	/praýs/	[prɑˈys̠]
μωϋσῆς	/moysés/	[mo̞yˈs̠e̞s̠]
προϋπῆρχον	/proypérxon/	[pro̞yˈpe̞rxo̞n]

In the Judeo-Palestinian Greek material, there is not much evidence for the pronunciation of *upsilon* with *diaeresis* until the Byzantine period (see *PNTG* §§8.1.6; 8.4.2): e.g., μωισης (for μωυσῆς) (*CIIP* 3211, 492–638 CE). Nevertheless, the above pronunciation conventions are probable for the Koine period.

> **ϋ around the Mediterranean**
>
> At the time of the New Testament, *upsilon* with *diaeresis* was likely pronounced separately from the preceding vowel. There is not much evidence for this in scribal conventions, though we do find interchanges like the following in Egypt: e.g., ιναρωουτος (for ἰναρωῦτος) (P.Hamb. 1.60, 90 CE).[131]

4.3.3 η–ηι (ῃ) (PNTG *§§8.1.2; 8.3.6*)

The vowel represented by η–ηι (ῃ) is pronounced similarly to *ey* in the English word *hey* but without the *y* that accompanies this sound in English—i.e., the Greek sound is not a diphthong. The difference between English and Greek here must be emphasized. English speakers have only a diphthong *ey* = [eɪ] at this place in the vowel space. Koine Greek, on the other hand, realizes the vowel η–ηι (ῃ) as a plain [e] without any trace of a diphthong. This can be a difficult sound for English speakers to learn to pronounce. To pronounce this sound correctly, a helpful exercise is to begin by holding the English sound *ey* (as in *hey*) for a long duration (e.g., several seconds). Then, try to replicate the vowel sound that is being held before getting to the end of the diphthong. The key is to notice yourself holding the sound without moving the articulators in your mouth. After you practice this several times so that you can isolate

131. Gignac, *Grammar of the Greek Papyri I*, 186–87.

the sound before the ending of the diphthong, pronounce that sound by itself for a normal duration. This simple vowel is called a close-mid front vowel (IPA /e/).

ἥλιος	/élios/	['eljọs]
σημεῖον	/semíon/	[seˈmiọn]
ἠλάμην	/elámen/	[eˈlamen]
ἔρχη	/érxe/	[ˈɛrxe]
εἴπη	/ípe/	[ˈipe]
δόξη	/ðókse/	[ˈðoksẹ]

In some other regional varieties during the Roman period (and in Modern Greek), the vowel η had already merged with ι–ει and was pronounced as a front close unrounded vowel /i/. This is its pronunciation in Modern Greek. Thus, if one wants greater similarity between their pronunciation and that of Modern Greek, it is acceptable historically (in some regional varieties) to pronounce η as ι–ει = /i/, even though this change was not carried through universally in General Koine until the Byzantine period.

ἥλιος	/ílios/	[ˈiʎọs]
σημεῖον	/simíon/	[siˈmiọn]
ἠλάμην	/ilámin/	[iˈlamin]
ἔρχη	/érxi/	[ˈɛrxi]
εἴπη	/ípi/	[ˈipi]
δόξη	/ðóksi/	[ˈðoksi]

There are two important developments to address in the Judeo-Palestinian Greek material with respect to η–ηι (η): (i) the monophthongization of ηι (η) and (ii) the eventual merger of η and ι.

In the Hellenistic period, the sequence ηι (η) is written as ηι roughly 74% of the time: e.g., ψυχηι (for ψυχῇ) (*CIIP* 2482, 3rd c. BCE), τηι τοιαυτηι (for τῇ τοιαύτῃ) (*CIIP* 3511, 178 BCE), τ]ηι γηι (for τῇ γῇ) (4Q119, 125–1 BCE); but cf. βουλη (for βούλῃ) (*CIIP* 3532, 225–175 BCE). By the first century, however, the orthography η is the overwhelming norm: e.g., εν τη (for ἐν τῇ) (8HevXIIgr, 50 BCE–50 CE); αν ληφθη (for ἂν ληφθῇ) (*CIIP* 2, 23 BCE–

70 CE) (*PNTG* §8.1.2.1). This suggests that monophthongization of ηι (η) had already taken place by the end of the Hellenistic period.

The merger of η and ι, on the other hand, is not widespread in Judeo-Palestinian Greek until the late Byzantine period. Although there are some η ↔ ι interchanges attested at an earlier period, η ↔ ε interchanges are much more common in the first century: e.g., δοτη (for δότε) (*CIIP* 1091, 1st c. CE); μησου (for μέσου) (Jer4, 132–135 CE) (*PNTG* §8.3.7.1). In fact, it is not until the sixth century CE that η ↔ ι interchanges come to be attested more frequently than η ↔ ε interchanges (*PNTG* §8.3.6.2.I). This demonstrates that /e/ was the majority pronunciation of η throughout the Roman period and even the early Byzantine period. In this respect, Judeo-Palestinian Koine is more conservative than other regional varieties of the Koine.

ηι (η) around the Mediterranean

At the time of the New Testament, essentially every regional variety of the Koine had already monophthongized ηι (η). In Attic inscriptions, ηι (η) was the first of the long diphthongs ending in ι to monophthongize (e.g., τη πολει for τῇ πόλει), beginning in the fourth or third century BCE.[132] In Egypt, the long diphthong ηι (η) underwent monophthongization by the middle of the third century BCE.[133] In both Anatolia and Italy, the long diphthong ηι (η) is already monophthongized in our Roman-period attestations.[134] After monophthongization, the pronunciation would likely follow the same absolute chronology as η did in each region.

η around the Mediterranean

At the time of the New Testament, while there were likely some pronunciation systems that had already merged η and ι (e.g., dialects in Asia Minor), most Koine speakers were still pronouncing η as /eː/ or /e/. In Attic

---

132. Threatte, *Grammar of Attic Inscriptions I*, 353–67.

133. Teodorsson, *Ptolemaic Koine*, 220–22.

134. Leon, "Jewish Catacombs"; Brixhe, *Grec anatolien*, 48–49; Brixhe, "Asia Minor," 232.

inscriptions, original η = [ɛˑ] slowly raised over the course of the Hellenistic period to [eˑ], which itself subsequently raised to and merged with ι = [i(ˑ)] around the latter part of the second century CE, though some speakers still maintained an [e(ˑ)] pronunciation.[135] In Egypt, the quality of η had raised from [ɛː] to [eː] by the end of the third century BCE; the subsequent merger with ι likely took place around the second century CE, though some speakers likely kept them distinct for some time after.[136] In Anatolia, the initial raising of η to [eː] is attested in Miletos by the third century BCE and in Magnesia by 200 BCE. The subsequent raising to [iː] is attested by the first century CE. The complete isochronous merger of η and ι is attested already by our second-century CE attestations.[137] In Italy, the data from the Jewish catacombs of Rome (ca. 2nd/3rd c. CE) appear to reflect a transitional period, during which most speakers pronounced η as [e] but a minority had already begun to pronounce η as [i].[138] In the provincial dialects of the east, it appears that η maintained its close-mid pronunciation of [e] well into the fifth and sixth centuries among some speakers.[139]

4.3.4 ε–αι (PNTG §§8.2.1; 8.3.7)

The vowel represented by ε–αι is pronounced like *e* in English *pet*. This is called an open-mid front unrounded vowel (IPA /ɛ/).

ἐγώ	/ɛγó/	[ɛˈɣo]
λέγει	/léγi/	[ˈlɛ̝i]
εἰπέ	/ipé/	[iˈpɛ]
ταῖς	/tés/	[ˈtɛs]
αἰνῶ	/ɛnó/	[ɛˈnọ]
γυναῖκα	/ɣynéka/	[ɟyˈnɛka]

135. Threatte, *Grammar of Attic Inscriptions I*, 159–71.

136. Gignac, *Grammar of the Greek Papyri I*, 235–49; Teodorsson, *Ptolemaic Koine*, 216–22.

137. Brixhe, *Grec anatolien*, 46–49; Brixhe, "Asia Minor," 232; Bubenik, *Hellenistic and Roman Greece*, 245.

138. Leon, "Jewish Catacombs," 213–16.

139. Bubenik, *Hellenistic and Roman Greece*, 238.

In the Judeo-Palestinian Greek material, interchanges of αι and ε begin already in the Hellenistic period but are not common until the beginning of the second century CE: e.g., ανετειως (for ἀναιτίως) (*CIIP* 3689, 200–150 BCE); σαβαθεου (for σαββαταίου) (*CIIP* 586, 1st c. BCE/CE); χερε (for χαῖρε) (*CIIP* Ap.4, 1st–2nd c. BCE/CE); τες προγεγραμμενες (for ταῖς προγεγραμμέναις) (5/6Hev15, 125 CE); χερειν (for χαίρειν) (XHev/Se64, 129 CE); συνκεχωρηκενε (for συγκεχωρηκέναι) (5/6Hev20, 130 CE) (*PNTG* §8.2.1.1.II). This likely indicates that the αι, ε → ε merger had begun among a minority of speakers in the Hellenistic period but came to be widespread at some point before the beginning of the second century CE.

While some scholars of Koine Greek phonology reconstruct the pronunciation of ε–αι as a true-mid vowel /ẹ/—this is its pronunciation in Modern Greek—its realization in Judeo-Palestinian Koine was probably a slightly more open /ε/. This realization is supported by the fact that Greek ε is normally rendered in loanwords in Hebrew with an /a/-vowel: e.g., ἐξέδρα → אַכְּסַדְרָה (ʔaχsaðra); σέλλα → סַלָּה (salla) (*PNTG* §8.3.7.5.I). It is likely, however, that after η merged with ι in the Byzantine period, the empty space on the front axis caused a minimal "pull" effect on ε = /ε/ so that it raised slightly in quality to /ẹ/ (see *PNTG* §8.3.7.7).

αι around the Mediterranean

At the time of the New Testament, the historical diphthong αι was in the process of undergoing monophthongization and eventually merging with ε. Because this process happened earlier in some regions than others, it is likely that one would have encountered some first-century Greek speakers pronouncing αι as /ai̯/ or /ae̯/, others pronouncing it as a long /æː/ or /εː/, and still others who were pronouncing it identically to ε = /ε/ (or /ẹ/). In Egypt, for example, the initial monophthongization of αι [ai̯] → [ae̯] → [æː] probably took place by the beginning of the second century BCE; after the onset of isochrony, this vowel then merged with ε = [ε] (or [ẹ]) probably by the end of the second century BCE: e.g., καλαμε πολλε (for καλάμαι πολλαί) (P.Lond. 7.2061, 3rd c. BCE); παλεου (for παλαιοῦ) (*UPZ* 1.94, 2nd c. BCE).[140] In Anatolia, the monophthongization of αι is attested by the first century BCE in Miletos and by the first century CE in Magnesia. By our second-

---

140. Edwin Mayser and Hans Schmoll, *Grammatik der griechischen Papyri aus*

century CE attestations, a complete merger with ε is clear. It should also be noted that some dialects in Anatolia appear to reflect a generally more close pronunciation of ε–αι as /ẹ/ or /e/: e.g., μηδινα (for μηδένα) and επο (for ὑπό).[141] In Attic inscriptions, the short diphthong αι likely monophthongized to ε = [ẹ] (via [æ(:)]) by around 125 CE.[142] In Italy, αι has clearly already merged with ε by our second-century CE attestations.[143]

4.3.5 α–αι (ᾳ) (PNTG §§8.1.1; 8.3.8)

The vowel represented by α–αι (ᾳ) is pronounced similarly to the *a* in English *mama* or *papa*.[144] This is called a back open unrounded vowel (IPA /ɑ/).

ἀγάπη	/aɣápe/	[aˈɣape]
λαγός	/laɣós/	[laˈɣọṣ]
θύρα	/θýra/	[ˈθyra]
ᾅδης	/áðes/	[ˈaðeṣ]
τῇ οἰκίᾳ	/té ykía/	[ˈte yˈcia]
ἐν ἡμέρᾳ	/ɛn eméra/	[ɛn eˈmɛra]

In the Judeo-Palestinian Greek material, the historically long diphthong ᾱι (ᾳ) can be written as αι in the Hellenistic period: e.g., [μαχαιρα]ι

der Ptolemäerzeit: Band 1: Laut- und Wortlehre (Berlin: de Gruyter, 1970), 83–87; Gignac, *Grammar of the Greek Papyri I*, 192–97; Teodorsson, *Ptolemaic Koine*, 222–25. Search also via the TM Text Irregularities database. See Depauw and Stolk, "Linguistic Variation."

141. Brixhe, *Grec anatolien*, 47; 53–55; Brixhe, "Asia Minor," 232–33; Bubenik, *Hellenistic and Roman Greece*, 245.

142. See Threatte, *Grammar of Attic Inscriptions I*, 268.

143. Leon, "Jewish Catacombs," 219–21.

144. See GreekPod101.com, "Greek Pronunciation - Vowels" (2015): accessed 26 October, 2021, https://youtu.be/Xql6qZ3lpUo.

(for [μαχαίρᾳ]) (4Q119, 125–1 BCE).[145] By the first century, however, historical ᾱι (ᾳ) is essentially written only as α: e.g., ο αδης (for ὁ ᾄδης) (8HevXIIgr, 50 BCE–50 CE); επ αδικια (for ἐπ᾽ ἀδικίᾳ) (NAZARETH, 27 BCE–14 CE). This suggests that monophthongization of ᾱι (ᾳ) had already taken place before the end of the Hellenistic period.

αι (ᾳ) around the Mediterranean

At the time of the New Testament, virtually all regional varieties of the Koine had already monophthongized αι (ᾳ). In Egypt, the historically long diphthong ᾱι (ᾳ) became monophthongized by the end of the third century BCE: e.g., πανοικια (for πανοικίᾳ) (*SB* 5.7524, 249 BCE); θραxος (for θραχός) (P.Col.Zen. 2.80, 246 BCE).[146] In Attic inscriptions, there is evidence that monophthongization of the long diphthong ᾱι (ᾳ) began in the second century BCE, notably a century or two after that of ηι (ῃ) but around the same time as ωι (ῳ).[147] In both Anatolia and Italy, the long diphthong ᾱι (ᾳ) is already monophthongized in our Roman-period attestations.[148]

4.3.6 ο–ω–ωι (ῳ) (PNTG §§8.1.3; 8.3.9–10)

The vowel represented by ο–ω–ωι (ῳ) is pronounced similarly to *o* in the American English word *note* but without the *u* that accompanies this sound in English—i.e., the Greek sound is not a diphthong. As was the case with η–ηι (ῃ), the corresponding English vowel in that part of the vowel space is only a diphthong *o* = [ου]. In Koine Greek, this sound should be pronounced as a plain *o* without any trace of a diphthong. Moreover, the Greek vowel is actually pronounced with a bit more open

---

145. For why this partially fragmentary word is an acceptable attestation, see *PNTG* §8.1.1.1.I.

146. Teodorsson, *Ptolemaic Koine*, 123, 222.

147. Threatte, *Grammar of Attic Inscriptions I*, 353–67.

148. Leon, "Jewish Catacombs"; Brixhe, *Grec anatolien*, 48–49; Brixhe, "Asia Minor," 232.

quality than English *o*. Spanish *o* would be a much better parallel. In phonetic terms, this is called a back true-mid rounded vowel (IPA /o̞/). To practice this sound, say a word like *note* (in American English) but hold the *o* sound for a long duration without saying the last part of the diphthong. The key is to notice yourself holding the sound without moving the articulators in your mouth. Practice this until you can isolate that sound by itself and then say it with a shorter duration. Now, create a bit more openness in your mouth as you are saying this vowel to get the Greek vowel quality right.

ὄνομα	/ónoma/	[ˈo̞no̞ma]
λόγος	/lóγos/	[ˈlo̞γo̞s]
θεός	/θeós/	[θeˈo̞s]
ὧδε	/óðe/	[ˈo̞ðɛ]
δίδωμι	/ðíðomi/	[ˈðiðo̞mi]
ἰδών	/iðón/	[iˈðo̞n]
τῷ λαῷ	/tó laó/	[ˈto̞ laˈo̞]
αὐτῷ	/aφtó/	[aˈφto̞]
δῷς	/ðós/	[ˈðo̞s]

As was the case above (cf. §4.3.3), there are two important developments to address in the Judeo-Palestinian Greek material with respect to o–ω–ωι (ῳ): (i) the monophthongization of ωι (ῳ) and (ii) the eventual merger of ω and o.

In the Hellenistic period, the sequence ωι (ῳ) is written as ωι roughly 78% of the time: e.g., τωι αδελφωι (for τῷ ἀδελφῷ) (*CIIP* 3511, 178 BCE); εν καιρωι (for ἐν καιρῷ) (4Q119, 125–1 BCE); but cf. επι αγαθω (for ἐπὶ ἀγαθῷ) (*CIIP* 3689, 200–150 BCE). Even though this conservative orthography lingers on well into the Roman period, the majority spelling is already ω: e.g., τινι τροπω (for τινὶ τρόπῳ) (NAZARETH, 27 BCE–14 CE), τω ξυλω (for τῷ ξύλῳ) (8HevXIIgr, 50 BCE–50 CE); but cf. εαυτωι (for ἑαυτῷ) (*CIIP* 2, 23 BCE–70 CE), τωι αδελφωι (for τῷ ἀδελφῷ) (5/6Hev59, 135 CE) (*PNTG* §8.1.3.1.I–II). This suggests that, although monophthongization of ωι (ῳ) likely occurred by the end of the Hellenistic period, it was probably later than that of ηι (ῃ) and αι (ᾳ) given the lingering prevalence of the convention ωι (ῳ) → ωι in the first century.

In the Judeo-Palestinian Greek material of the Hellenistic period, there are already frequent interchanges of ω → o, though they tend to be in texts typically associated with less educated scribes (graffiti, domestic inscriptions, etc.): e.g., γεροvιος (for γερώvιος) (*CIIP* 3466, 332–150 BCE); ηλιωδορου (for ἡλιοδώρου) (*CIIP* 3674, 143/142 BCE); βασιλεος (for βασιλέως) (*CIIP* 3731, 332–40 BCE) (*PNTG* §8.3.10.1). At the very least this reflects an identity in quality between ω and o in the Hellenistic period, but it likely also indicates that the merger of ω, o → o had already begun among a segment of the Judeo-Palestinian population in Hellenistic times. Such interchanges continue to be attested in the first century: e.g., πολεος (for πόλεως) (*CIIP* 1732, 1st c. BCE/CE); πολεος (for πόλεως) (*CIIP* 579, 1st c. BCE/CE); αποδοσο (for ἀποδώσω) (EinGedi1, 75–135 CE) (*PNTG* §8.3.10.1). Therefore, the complete merger of ω and o would depend on whether a particular group of speakers was still maintaining phonemic length distinctions in the vowel system. Because the first century marks the transition point from a system with phonemic length to one characterized by isochrony in Judeo-Palestinian Greek (see §4.3.8), there were likely some speakers who still pronounced ω as [o̞ː] and others who had completely merged ω and o to [o̞] at the time of the New Testament.

ωι (ῳ) around the Mediterranean

At the time of the New Testament, the various regional varieties of the Koine all seem to have already monophthongized ωι (ῳ). In Egypt, the long diphthong ωι (ῳ) became monophthongized by the end of the third century BCE: e.g., ετοιμω (for ἑτοίμῳ) (P.Hib. 2.253, ca. 250 BCE).[149] In Attic inscriptions, there is evidence that monophthongization of the long diphthong ωι (ῳ) began in the second century BCE, notably a century or two after that of ηι (ῃ) but around the same time as ᾱι (ᾳ).[150] In both Anatolia and Italy, the long diphthong ωι (ῳ) is already monophthongized in our Roman-period attestations.[151]

---

149. Teodorsson, *Ptolemaic Koine*, 161–62; 234–36. Search also via Papyri.info.
150. Threatte, *Grammar of Attic Inscriptions I*, 353–67.
151. Leon, "Jewish Catacombs"; Brixhe, *Grec anatolien*, 48–49; Brixhe, "Asia Minor," 232.

ω around the Mediterranean

At the time of the New Testament, most speakers of Koine Greek probably pronounced ω with the same vocalic quality as o. Speakers who used a more conservative pronunciation system with phonemic length likely pronounced the former as [ọ:] and the latter as [ọ]. Speakers who used a more innovative pronunciation characterized by isochrony likely pronounced both identically as [ọ]. Because the onset of isochrony occurred at different times in different regions, there was likely considerable variation in the first century with respect to the pronunciation of ω. In Egypt, the initial shift of [ɔ:] → [ọ:] had reached completion by the third century BCE; the subsequent merger of ω and o likely occurred by the end of the second century BCE.[152] In Attic inscriptions, the quality of ω (originally = /ɔ:/) approached that of o (/ọ/) already in the fourth century BCE. However, it was likely not until around 150 CE—when quantitative distinctions in vowel length were lost—that ω and o fully merged.[153] Anatolia exhibits a clear merger of ω and o by our second- and third-century CE epigraphic attestations.[154] Although the evidence from the Jewish catacombs of Rome has been interpreted as reflecting a more close ω and a more open o, the data appear sufficient to conclude that ω has merged with o by our second- and third-century CE attestations.[155]

4.3.7 ου (PNTG §8.3.11)

The vowel represented by ου is pronounced like *oo* in English *loot*. This is called a back close rounded vowel (IPA /u/).

οὐρανός	/uraˈnós/	[uraˈnọs]
τοῦτο	/túto/	[ˈtutọ]
αὐτοῦ	/aφtú/	[aˈφtu]

152. Gignac, *Grammar of the Greek Papyri I*, 275–77; Teodorsson, *Ptolemaic Koine*, 233–36.

153. Threatte, *Grammar of Attic Inscriptions I*, 223–33.

154. Brixhe, *Grec anatolien*, 47; Brixhe, "Asia Minor," 232.

155. Leon, "Jewish Catacombs," 217–18.

4.3.8 Vowel Length (PNTG §8.6.1)

In Classical Greek and Great Attic, vowel length (or quantity) was phonemic. This means that holding a vowel sound for longer—typically anywhere from 1.2x–2.5x longer than the duration of a short vowel—was an essential feature of its pronunciation and necessary for conveying proper meaning.[156] In the "common" or innovative (nonconservative) register of the Roman period, however, vowels were no longer distinguished by length. As such, historically long vowels (i.e., ī, ū, η, ᾱ, ω) were no longer distinguished from short vowels by phonemic quantity. Rather, they were distinguished, if at all, only by quality. As such, etymologically long ī is pronounced the same as etymologically short ĭ, ᾱ the same as ᾰ, and ω the same as ο.

δῷς ('give.SUBJ') vs.	/ðós/	[ˈðos]
δός ('give.IMPV')		
κρῑθή ('barley.NOUN') vs.	/kriθé/	[kriˈθe]
κρῐθῇ ('be judged.SUBJ')		
κᾰθᾰρά ('clean-FSG') vs.	/kaθará/	[kaθaˈra]
κᾰθᾰρᾰ́ ('clean-NPL')		

In the Judeo-Palestinian Greek material, there are four primary interchanges that reflect the onset of isochrony: αι → ε, ω → ο, η → ε, and -ιος#/-ιον# → -ις#/-ιν# (see *PNTG* §8.6.1.1). Conversely, there is one particular interchange by which the scribe indicates phonemic (or etymological) length: ī → ει (see *PNTG* §§8.3.2.1.I; 8.6.1.1).

The former interchanges (i.e., those reflecting isochrony) all begin in the Hellenistic period but gradually increase in frequency until they (for the most part) reach their height at the end of the late Roman period, after which time they continue to be attested at roughly the same rate for the rest of the Byzantine period.[157] This suggests that isochrony be-

---

156. Words like κᾰθᾰρᾰ́ 'clean-NOM.FSG' and κᾰθᾰρᾰ́ 'clean-NOM.NPL', for example, would have been distinguished only by the duration of the final vowel: [katʰaraá] 'clean-NOM.FSG' as opposed to [katʰará] 'clean-NOM.NPL'.

157. This is based on averaging the relative attestation rates of the interchanges

gan among a small portion of the population in the Hellenistic period, became more widespread during the early Roman period, and became the norm by the late Roman period.

The latter interchange (i.e., that reflecting phonemic length) gains popularity as a "Roman" scribal convention (imported to Judea-Palestine) around the beginning of the first century. It reaches its peak by the end of the early Roman period before starting to taper off in the late Roman period and then becoming relatively unsubstantial in the Byzantine period. This suggests that there was a more conservative pronunciation system with phonemic vowel length and that, in some form or another, this was maintained as late as the third century CE.

What does this mean, then, for the situation in the first century? At the time of the New Testament, significant segments of the population in Judea-Palestine were already speaking with an isochronous vowel system. At the same time, a more conservative pronunciation system existed in which vowel length distinctions were still phonemic. It is plausible that both pronunciations were mainstream and coexisted during the first century. There is some evidence that the more conservative pronunciation was associated with higher levels of education and/or more formal registers (see discussion in *PNTG* §§8.3.2.1.I; 9.2), but this may be only one factor among many. In the late Roman period, however, the preservation of phonemic vowel length was almost certainly a minority—and in many cases learned—pronunciation. The early Roman period (ca. 37 BCE–135 CE) thus marks the key transition period in Judeo-Palestinian Greek from a system with phonemic length to a system with isochrony. By the end of the second century CE, isochrony seems to have become the norm.

Vowel Length around the Mediterranean

At the time of the New Testament, one could encounter around the Mediterranean world both Greek speakers who maintained phonemic length

---

associated with isochrony. See Figure 8.25 in *PNTG* §8.6.1.1. Note, however, that certain individual interchanges associated with isochrony (e.g., ω → o) may still exhibit increases in frequency in the late Byzantine period. See Figure 8.24 in *PNTG* §8.6.1.1.

distinctions and Greek speakers whose vowel systems were isochronous. While the division between these two types of speakers was sometimes merely regional or dialectal, in other cases it was sociolinguistic. The pronunciation system with phonemic length distinctions was regarded as more prestigious and more fitting for speeches, songs, poems, etc. Therefore, it is even possible that some speakers might have used an isochronous pronunciation system in their everday speech but attempted to use a pronunciation system with phonemic length distinctions in the art of rhetoric.

Despite the relevance of sociolinguistics, there are nevertheless certain important regional differences to be considered with respect to the onset of isochrony. An isochronous pronunciation system seems to be first attested in Egypt around the third or second century BCE, which is likely due to the fact that Egypt shifted from a pitch accent to a stress accent earlier than other regional varieties.[158] Anatolian Koine—at least certain dialects within Anatolia—seems to have been the next regional variety to adopt isochrony on a wide scale, perhaps around the third or second century BCE.[159] In Italy, the Jewish inscriptions of the catacombs appear to reflect a situation in which isochrony had become prevalent in common speech by the second century CE (at the latest).[160] While some regions in Greece exhibit isochrony as early as the first century BCE, it generally began in the first century CE and became widespread by the second century CE.[161]

158. Horrocks, *Greek*, 122n5, 129, 164–70; José Antonio Berenguer-Sánchez and Juan Rodríguez Somolinos, "Sur la flexion nominale en -ις, -ιν," in *Papyrologica Vindobonensia. Akten des 23. Internationalen Papyrologenkongresses. 1* (Vienna: Verlag der Österreichischen Akademie der Wissenschaften, 2007), 44.

159. Claude Brixhe, "Le changement <IO> → <I> en pamphylien, en laconien et dans la koiné d'Egypte," *Verbum* 16 (1994): 219–41; Berenguer-Sánchez and Somolinos, "Flexion nominale," 39. Miletos exhibits isolated examples of nonpreservation of length in the third century BCE. In Magnesia and Priene, quantity is no longer maintained from the second century BCE. See Bubenik, *Hellenistic and Roman Greece*, 245. The Anatolian inscriptions of the Roman period exhibit a highly progressed system in which η has merged with ι and all vowel length distinctions are lost. See Brixhe, *Grec anatolien*, 46–49; Brixhe, "Asia Minor," 232.

160. Leon, "Jewish Catacombs," 211, 216.

161. In light of the -ιος#/-ιον# → -ις#/-ιν# shift, Laconia might have become isochronous already in the first century BCE. See Brixhe, "Changement <IO> → <I>"; Berenguer-Sánchez and Somolinos, "Flexion nominale," 39. In inscriptional Attic,

In some of these very same regions, however, and precisely during those periods in which isochrony is said to have prevailed, we find evidence of preserved phonemic length. In Asia Minor, for example, the first- or second-century CE Seikilos epitaph, which was found near Ephesus, appears to make use of phonemic length and pitch accent, albeit in a musical context.[162] Similarly, we find the second-century CE Latin grammarian and author Terentianus Maurus writing Greek words mapped onto Latin meter with correct length.[163] Finally, the Latin grammarian Velius Longus (2nd c. CE) describes the Greek vowels as having phonemic length.[164]

The tension between these two seemingly contradictory strands of evidence may best be summed up in Philostratus's statement about the Athens-trained (by Herodes Atticus) second-century CE Cappadocian rhetorician Pausanias of Caesarea, whom he ridicules for not pronouncing length correctly:[165] "Even though he had attained to much of the excellencies of Herodes (his teacher), and especially the ability to orate extemporaneously, he would deliver [his speeches] with coarse accent, even as is customary for the Cappadocians, on one hand, running together the

---

there is "conclusive evidence of vowel isochrony" beginning in the Roman period, most notably after 100 CE: e.g., απολλωνει (for ἀπόλλωνϊ) (54–68 CE); αλοχο (for ἀλόχῳ) (ca. 150 CE). See Threatte, *Grammar of Attic Inscriptions I*, 385–87. For isochrony in Delphi and Magnesia, see Edmund Rüsch, *Grammatik der delphischen Inschriften. I. Lautlehre* (Berlin: Weidmannsche Buchhandlung, 1914), 76, 144–47; and E. Nachmanson, *Laute und Formen der magnetischen Inschriften* (Uppsala: Almqvist & Wiksells, 1904), 63–65.

162. See Jon Solomon, "The Seikilos Inscription: A Theoretical Analysis," *American Journal of Philology* 107, no. 4 (1986): 455–79.

163. See Terentianus Maurus, *De litteris, de syllabis, de metris*. I would like to thank Luke Ranieri for drawing this to my attention.

164. *De Orthographia*: 47. See Heinrich Keil, *Velius Longus: De Orthographia* (Leipzig: Teubner, 1880).

165. *Vitae sophistarum* 2.594.6–9: ἐς πολλὰ δὲ ἀναφέρων τῶν Ἡρώδου πλεονεκτημάτων καὶ μάλιστα τὸ αὐτοσχεδιάζειν· ἀπήγγελλε δὲ αὐτὰ παχείᾳ τῇ γλώττῃ καὶ ὡς Καππαδόκαις ξύνηθες, ξυγκρούων μὲν τὰ σύμφωνα τῶν στοιχείων, συστέλλων δὲ τὰ μηκυνόμενα καὶ μηκύνων τὰ βραχέα. See Wilmer Cave Wright, *Philostratus, the Lives of the Sophists; Eunapius, Lives of the Philosophers*, Loeb Classical Library 134 (Cambridge: Harvard University Press, 2015). See also Schweizer, *Grammatik der pergamenischen Inschriften*, 94–96.

consonantal sounds, and on the other hand, shortening long syllables and lengthening short syllables."

This quotation illustrates what was likely the situation in many regional varieties of the Koine during the Roman period. In everyday speech, many (or most) speakers operated within an isochronous vowel system. In more formal settings—music, speeches, poems, literature, etc.—there was an expectation for one to speak with proper phonemic length distinctions. Both pronunciation systems thus existed side-by-side and were used in different contexts, though the system with phonemic length distinctions might sometimes have been more artificial. In fact, if we look closely at the content of the Seikilos epitaph, there are good reasons—such as the rhyming of ζῆν 'to live' and ἀπαιτεῖ 'demands in return'—for regarding the apparent use of vowel length and pitch accent as "archaizing" and not as an authentic reflection of contemporary colloquial speech.[166]

4.3.9 *Accents and Stress* (PNTG §8.6.2)

The term *accent* is used to refer to the giving of prominence to a particular syllable (or mora) in a word. Among the languages of the world, there are two main types of word accent. The first, which is known as *pitch accent*, involves changing the frequency of vibration of the vocal cords so that a particular syllable sounds higher or lower. The second, which is known as *stress accent*, typically involves a greater exertion of pressure in articulation, a greater duration of length, and (sometimes) also a change in pitch. These two systems are not mutually exclusive in terms of marking prominence (or "accent") in a language, but it is possible to

166. Note that the rhyme of ζῆν and ἀπαιτεῖ implies that Greek η had already merged with ι-ει = /i/, which would not generally have been characteristic of a pronunciation system with phonemic vowel length. I would like to thank Armand D'Angour, a world-leading scholar of ancient Greek music at Jesus College, Oxford, for pointing this out to me and explaining that the author was likely "archaizing." See also Armand D'Angour, "Musica Linguae, Lingua Musicae" (presentation, Classics in Praxis at Delphi Economic Forum VII, Delphi, Greece, April 8, 2022); transcript available at https://www.armand-dangour.com/2022/04/musica-linguae-lingua-musicae/.

have one without the other. When they occur together, pitch and stress do not have to occur on the same syllable.[167] While the Classical accent system was ultimately based on pitch, at some point in the Koine period this pitch-based system began to shift to a stress-based system, or at least to acquire certain features thereof. Nevertheless, even the Neohellenic (Modern Greek) accent system, which largely coordinates with stress, has elements of pitch.[168]

The pronunciation recommended in this book is a stress-based accent system like Modern Greek. Syllables marked with an acute (ά) or circumflex accent (ᾶ) should be pronounced with slightly greater strength/volume, slightly longer duration, and a higher pitch.[169] While many cases of the grave accent (ὰ) should be pronounced in the same way, it is probably the case that short words with grave accents ran together with the following word. For example, τὸν ἄρτον might have been pronounced in the Koine period as [to̞'narto̞n], whereas τῶν ἄρτων might have been pronounced as ['to̞n 'arto̞n]. It should go without saying that pronouncing Greek stress is essential for understanding and appreciating the correct meaning of a particular word. For example, we can discern contrasts in the following words only by pronouncing them with proper stress (word stress is marked with ´ on the stressed vowel in phonemic representation and with IPA ' preceding the stressed syllable in phonetic representation).[170]

ἄγων 'leading'	/áɣon/	['aɣo̞n]
ἀγών 'competition'	/aɣón/	[a'ɣo̞n]
εἶπε 'said'	/ípɛ/	['ipɛ]

167. David Goldstein, "Pitch," in *Encyclopedia of Ancient Greek Language and Linguistics*, ed. Georgios K. Giannakis et al. (Leiden: Brill, 2014), 100–101; Chris Golston, "Stress," in *Encyclopedia of Ancient Greek Language and Linguistics*, ed. Georgios K. Giannakis et al. (Leiden: Brill, 2014), https://referenceworks.brillonline.com/browse/encyclopedia-of-ancient-greek-language-and-linguistics.

168. See Zachariou, *Pronouncing Biblical Greek*, 117–18.

169. See Holton, Mackridge, and Philippaki-Warburton, *Greek*, 28; and Zachariou, *Pronouncing Biblical Greek*, 116–18.

170. See Zachariou, *Pronouncing Biblical Greek*, 118 for a helpful list of words distinguished only by stress.

εἰπέ 'say!'	/ipé/	[iˈpɛ]
νόμος 'law'	/nómos/	[ˈnǫmǫs̩]
νομός 'district'	/nomós/	[nǫˈmǫs̩]

In the Judeo-Palestinian Greek material, the shift from a pitch-based accent system to a stress-based accent system can be discerned from the phonological and chronological distribution of certain spelling interchanges. For example, one sign that a pitch system has given way to (or has acquired features of) a stress system is that interchanges reflecting "lengthening" (i.e., ο → ω, ε → η, ῐ → ει) tend to occur more frequently in stressed syllables whereas interchanges reflecting "shortening" tend to occur more frequently in unstressed syllables (i.e., ω → ο, η → ε). Just such a distribution is characteristic of the early Roman period in Judea-Palestine, which suggests that the shift from a pitch accent to a stress accent occurred by the end of the Hellenistic period. It is likely that this development was then followed by the onset of isochrony (for more details on the shift from pitch to stress accent, see *PNTG* §8.6.2).

Pitch and Stress around the Mediterranean

In the everyday speech of many (or most) Greek speakers at the time of the New Testament, the accent system was probably based on (or at least had acquired features of) stress. Nevertheless, pronunciation systems with pitch accent would have been preserved at the very least for certain formal settings and high register contexts (see §4.3.8). In both Attica and Egypt during the Hellenistic period (4th–1st c. BCE), there is a slightly greater tendency for "long" vocalic graphemes to substitute for "short" vocalic graphemes in stressed syllables and for "short" vocalic graphemes to substitute for "long" vocalic graphemes in unstressed syllables. This likely indicates that the high pitch accent had acquired or was acquiring features of a stress accent, such as longer duration, during these centuries. It likely also indicates that the shift from a pitch accent to a stress accent preceded the onset of isochrony.[171]

---

171. Andrew M. Devine and Lawrence D. Stephens, *The Prosody of Greek Speech* (Oxford: Oxford University Press, 1994), 217–18.

4.4 Summary of Historical Koine Greek Pronunciation

A summary of the historical Koine Greek pronunciation system described in this book is outlined below with specific allophonic realizations noted according to phonological environment. For a detailed explanation of each letter and sound correspondence, see the relevant sections above.

TABLE 4.4-1: CONSONANTS OF HISTORICAL KOINE GREEK PRONUNCIATION

LETTER	PHONEME	ALLOPHONES	EXAMPLES
γ	/ɣ/	[ɣ]	γάμος
		[j] _ι,υ,η,ε (before front vowels)	ἐγένετο
		[g] γ,ν_ (after nasals)	φέγγος
		[ɟ] γ,ν_ι,υ,η,ε (before front vowels + after nasals)	ἄγγελος
		[ŋ] _μ (before /m/)	πρᾶγμα
β	/β/	[β]	βασιλεύς
		[b] μ,ν_ (after nasals)	λαμβάνω
δ	/ð/	[ð]	δοῦλος
		[d] ν_ (after nasals)	δένδρον
χ	/x/	[x]	χάρις
		[ç] _ι,υ,η,ε (before front vowels)	χαῖρε
φ	/φ/	[φ]	φωνή
θ	/θ/	[θ]	θεός
ʾ	—	—	ὁ
κ	/k/	[k]	καλός
		[c] _ι,υ,η,ε (before front vowels)	κεῖται
		[g] γ,ν_ (after nasals)	ἀγκάλαις
		[ɟ] γ,ν_ι,υ,η,ε (before front vowels + after nasals)	ἀνάγκη
		[g] ἐκ(-)_β,γ,δ,ζ,λ,μ,ν,ρ (in ἐκ(-) before voiced consonants)	ἐκ μέρους

LETTER	PHONEME	ALLOPHONES	EXAMPLES
π	/p/	[p]	ποιεῖν
		[b] μ,ν_ (after nasals)	τὴν πόλιν
τ	/t/	[t]	τέλος
		[d] ν_ (after nasals)	πέντε
μ	/m/	[m]	μόνος
		[(m)]_β,π (before stops)	πέμπω
ν	/n/	[n]	νόμος
		[(n)]_β,π,δ,τ (before nonvelar stops)	ἄνδρα
		[(ŋ)]¹⁷² (with γ)_γ,κ,χ,ξ (before velars)	ἀγκάλαις
		[(ɲ)]¹⁷³ (with γ)_γ,κ,χ+ι,υ,η,ε (before velars + front vowels)	ἀνάγκη
λ	/l/	[l]	λόγος
ρ	/r/	[r]	ῥῆμα
σ	/s/	[s]	σύ
		[z]_β,γ,δ,ζ,λ,μ,ν,ρ (before voiced consonants)	κόσμος
ζ	/z/	[z]	ζωή
ψ	/ps/	[ps]	ψυχή
		[bs] μ,ν_ (after nasals)	ἔπεμψα
ξ	/ks/	[ks]	ξύλον
		[gs] γ,ν_ (after nasals)	ἔλεγξον

172. But note that this weakening was less likely before χ.
173. See previous footnote.

TABLE 4.4-2: DIPHTHONGS OF HISTORICAL KOINE GREEK PRONUNCIATION

LETTER	PHONEME	ALLOPHONES	EXAMPLES
αυ	/aβ/	[αβ] _β,γ,δ,ζ,λ,μ,ν,ρ,V (before voiced consonants or vowels)	αὐλή
	/aφ/	[αφ] _θ,κ,ξ,π,σ,τ,φ,χ,ψ,# (before voiceless consonants or word end)	αὐτός
ευ	/εβ/	[εβ] _β,γ,δ,ζ,λ,μ,ν,ρ,V (before voiced consonants or vowels)	εὐαγγέλιον
	/εφ/	[εφ] _θ,κ,ξ,π,σ,τ,φ,χ,ψ,# (before voiceless consonants or word end)	εὐθέως
ηυ	/eβ/	[eβ] _β,γ,δ,ζ,λ,μ,ν,ρ,V (before voiced consonants or vowels)	ηὐδόκησεν
	/eφ/	[eφ] _θ,κ,ξ,π,σ,τ,φ,χ,ψ,# (before voiceless consonants or word end)	ηὐχόμην
υι	/y/	[y]	υἱός, εἰδυῖα
	/yi̯/	[yi̯] (commonly attested variant pronunciation in Roman period)	υἱός, εἰδυῖα

TABLE 4.4-3: VOWELS OF HISTORICAL KOINE GREEK PRONUNCIATION

LETTER	PHONEME	ALLOPHONES	EXAMPLES
ι, ει	/i/	[i]	λίθος, εἶπεν
		[j] #,β,γ,δ,ζ,λ,μ,ν,ρ,_υ,η,ε,α,ο,ου (for details, see §4.3.1)	δηνάριον, ἰατρός
		[ç] θ,κ,ξ,π,σ,τ,φ,χ,ψ_υ,η,ε,α,ο,ου (for details, see §4.3.1)	ἱμάτιον
υ, οι	/y/	[y]	ὕδωρ, οἶδα
η, ῃ	/e/	[e]	ἥλιος, ἔρχῃ
ε, αι	/ε/	[ε]	ἐγώ, αἰνῶ
α, ᾳ	/a/	[a]	ἀγάπη, ᾅδης
ο, ω, ῳ	/o/	[ǫ]	ὄνομα, ὧδε, αὐτῷ
ου	/u/	[u]	οὐρανός

5

How Should Greek Be Pronounced in the Classroom Tomorrow?

5.1 INTRODUCTION: DOES PRONUNCIATION REALLY MATTER?

At the end of the day, everyone learning and teaching New Testament Greek ultimately has the same goal: to read and understand the text of the New Testament. When faced with questions of pronunciation, however, many fail to see the importance of using a proper historical pronunciation, sounding the common refrain that "pronunciation doesn't really matter." It is the contention of this brief final chapter that giving careful attention to pronunciation is not only helpful, but *essential* for proper understanding, interpretation, exegesis, and experience of the text of the New Testament. In the rest of this chapter, we look at five reasons why this is the case, giving attention to the literature on Second Language Acquisition (SLA) where appropriate.

5.2 IF PRONUNCIATION DOESN'T MATTER, THEN LANGUAGE DOESN'T MATTER

One of the first things learned in an introduction to linguistics course is the relationship between the six basic levels of linguistic structure. At the center is *phonetics* (mere sounds), next is *phonology* (sounds that make meaning), next is *morphology* (sequences of sounds that help form words), next is *syntax* (the grammatical relationship of words to one another in forming phrases and sentences), next is *semantics* (the "literal" meaning of the phrases and sentences), and finally *pragmatics* (the actual/on-the-ground meaning in context).

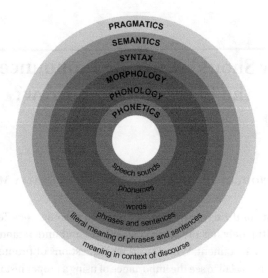

In the figure above, the outer concentric circles depend on the inner concentric circles. For example, one cannot properly infer pragmatics without first understanding semantics and syntax. Nor can one properly interpret syntax without first controlling morphology. Finally, one cannot properly analyze morphology without first grasping phonology and phonetics.s

Although we often tend to take the three innermost circles (morphology, phonology, phonetics) as given—syntax, semantics, and pragmatics are where real interpretive and exegetical work occurs—malpractice in the latter can often be the result of a failure to properly understand the former. For example, the choice of a FUT.IND-1CPL form in the phrase εἰ πατάξομεν ἐν μαχαίρᾳ; '*should* we strike with the sword?' (Luke 22:49) might seem odd when we are used to SUBJ forms expressing modal ideas.[1] While there are legitimate interpretive questions to ask about the rela-

1. See F. Blass, A. Debrunner, and Robert W. Funk, *A Greek Grammar of the New Testament and Other Early Christian Literature* (Cambridge/Chicago: Cambridge University Press/University of Chicago Press, 1961), §366.

tionship between morphology, semantics, and pragmatics in such a context, the relevance of pronunciation should not be ignored either. By the Roman period, many regional varieties of the Koine had already merged o and ω so that there would be no distinction in pronunciation between πατάξομεν FUT.IND-1CPL and πατάξωμεν AOR.SUBJ-1CPL. Speakers would have distinguished such forms only by syntactic patterning and other contextual clues—spelling would have been irrelevant, since most Koine Greek speakers who experienced the text would not have read it. If you are already using a Koine Greek pronunciation, then you are likely to process this text in the same way that the ancients did and perhaps feel some of the overlap of FUT.IND and AOR.SUBJ that the ancients sometimes did.

Indeed, because phonology ultimately determines the sounds that speakers find contrastive and thus forms the building blocks of meaning, the only way our processing of the language will work similarly to that of ancient native speakers is if we have the same type of meaningful sound contrasts that they did. If, for example, we pronounce o and ω distinctly—o as [ɔ] and ω as [oʊ]—as modern American "Erasmian" does, we will perceive certain phonemic contrasts that were not there for many speakers of Koine Greek. If, on the other hand, we pronounce η and ει identically—both as [e] or [eɪ]—as modern American "Erasmian" does, we will not feel the contrasts between φιλεῖ PRES.IND (Koine [ɸiˈli]) and φιλῇ PRES.SUBJ (Koine [ɸiˈle]) as an ancient Koine Greek speaker would have. If processing the language in the way the ancients did is important, then pronunciation is important.

5.3 Vocabulary Acquisition and Retention

Almost inevitably where "Erasmian" pronunciation is used, there tends to be very little care given to correct pronunciation of accents or stress. Maybe it goes back to the confusion introduced into the English-speaking world when Vossius (1618–1689) and Henning (1635–1684) claimed that Greek should be accented like Latin. Maybe the considerable emphasis put on "Erasmian" pronunciation corresponding perfectly with traditional spelling takes the focus away from the actual pronunciation. Maybe it is for another reason altogether. Such a neglect of Greek word stress by no means has to be the case, but for whatever reason classrooms using "Erasmian" pronunciation are notorious for not stressing Greek words correctly.[2] More emphasis is often put on remembering where to write the accent than on actually pronouncing the word stress correctly.[3] When there is no exact and consistent pronunciation of a word to be imitated, students do not process or remember their Greek vocabulary as real words in the way that they do the words of their native languages. One unfortunate result of such practice is that Greek vocabulary words are often identified with a visual conglomeration of certain letters rather than as an exact sequence of phonemes in a pattern with a distinct sound and shape. It is for this reason that students will often mistake words like λαθεῖν 'to escape notice' for ἐλθεῖν 'to come'.

Numerous SLA studies have shown that giving careful attention to pronunciation and word stress leads to more successful learning of vocabulary words among students. In a study of vocabulary learning among university students in China, Zhang and Lu found that strategies geared toward giving careful attention to the form of a word (i.e., spelling and pronunciation) were more successful than other learning strategies, noting that "if the form of a word is not in a learner's mental lexicon, it is not possible for the learner to connect other types of vocabulary knowledge to the word form. Therefore, studying word forms such as spelling and pronunciation is a prerequisite for building and expanding vocabulary size."[4] In a study of English for specific purposes (ESP) learners' reactions to vocabulary teaching strategies, Murphy found that "learners who are able to recognize and remember stress patterns feel more confident when

2. This same trend was already observed more than twenty-five years ago in Chrys C. Caragounis, "The Error of Erasmus and Un-Greek Pronunciations of Greek," *Filologia Neotestamentaria* 8 (1995): 182. There are professors of New Testament Greek, however, who would prove exceptions to this trend. I have heard that D. A. Carson, for example, makes it a point to insist on proper pronunciation of word stress when reading New Testament Greek. All who follow this example should be commended.

3. Admittedly, such generalization is largely based on anecdotal evidence and by no means applies to all classrooms that use "Erasmian" pronunciation. Nevertheless, I think most who start to pay attention to this issue will come to similar conclusions unless they are observing very exceptional classrooms.

4. Xian Zhang and Xiaofei Lu, "The Relationship between Vocabulary Learning Strategies and Breadth and Depth of Vocabulary Knowledge," *Modern Language Journal* 99, no. 4 (2015): 746–51.

using new vocabulary . . . [and] are more likely to be able to access such words from the mental lexicon."[5] The work of Fay and Cutler has shown that "syllable recognition and stress recognition must play the most important roles in decoding what has been said, and accessing meanings in the [mental] lexicon."[6] Indeed, Channell argues that "presentation of vocabulary should pay specific attention to pronunciation, in particular to word stress . . . visual presentation and reading may not be the best ways to introduce new vocabulary." Word stress and syllables are, in fact, high-level organizers of the mental lexicon.[7] The admitted overuse of quotations in this paragraph has hopefully driven home the point that correct pronunciation and word stress are not only indispensable but probably the most important parts of learning new vocabulary.

While those who use the "Erasmian" pronunciation could achieve similar outcomes with respect to vocabulary by insisting on proper word stress—there are, of course, exceptional classrooms that do—it would be hard to deny that those using a Neohellenic (Modern) Greek or Koine Greek pronunciation tend to be much more consistent with word stress than those using an "Erasmian" pronunciation. Part of this may be due to the similarity to and/or interface with Modern Greek, in which the pronunciation of correct word stress is consistently observed.

5.4 Fluent Reading:
"It Just Sounds More Like a Real Language"

Anecdotally, many students of New Testament Greek who adopt a Neohellenic or Koine Greek pronunciation system notice an immediate impact on their reading experience. It becomes more natural and fluent. "It just sounds more like a real language," they say. Some of the more erudite

5. John Murphy, "Attending to Word-Stress While Learning New Vocabulary," *English for Specific Purposes* 23, no. 1 (2004): 67–83.

6. D. Fay and A. Cutler, "Malapropisms and the Structure of the Mental Lexicon," *Linguistic Inquiry* 8, no. 3 (1977): 505–20; Joanna M. Channell, "Vocabulary Acquisition and the Mental Lexicon," in *Meaning and Lexicography*, ed. Jerzy Tomaszczyk and Barbara Lewandowska-Tomaszczyk (Philadelphia: John Benjamins, 1990), 26.

7. Channell, "Vocabulary Acquisition," 28–29.

among us might respond by regarding all such aesthetic judgments as merely subjective and culturally conditioned, but is that really the case? Is there no scientific or linguistic explanation for why New Testament Greek readers experience greater fluency by adopting a historically authentic—whether Neohellenic or Koine—Greek pronunciation?

There is, in fact, empirical evidence that would justify this otherwise seemingly subjective experience. Even though every language is different, there are certain general tendencies that seem to apply fairly extensively across the spectrum of the world's languages, whether these tendencies may be explained in light of the concept of Universal Grammar (UG) or in light of other considerations.[8] As it applies to phonology, we might say that there are certain phonemic inventories (i.e., the collection of vowels and consonants) that are more common among the world's languages, those that are less common, and those that are seemingly unattested. As it turns out, the phonemic and phonetic inventory implied by a fairly mainstream American "Erasmian" pronunciation advocated by a number of popular textbooks of New Testament Greek has at least a few features that we would not typically expect to find among the world's languages and/or are internally inconsistent.[9]

> The vocalic inventory of a mainstream American "Erasmian" includes five simple vowels /i/, /ε/, /ɑ/, /ɔ/, /u/ and five or seven diphthongs /eɪ/, /aɪ/, /aʊ/, /ɔɪ/, /oʊ/ (and possibly /ju/, /wi/). The diphthongs are comprised mostly of vowel and/or consonant sounds that are not otherwise phonemes by themselves.

8. Larry Hyman, "Universals in Phonology," *Linguistic Review* 25, no. 1–2 (2008): 345–90; Brett Miller, Neil Myler, and Bert Vaux, "Phonology in Universal Grammar," in *The Oxford Handbook of Universal Grammar*, ed. Ian Roberts (Oxford: Oxford University Press, 2016), 153–82.

9. Although there is some variation regarding the pronunciation of ζ, the other issues occur in numerous popular New Testament Greek textbooks: e.g., William D. Mounce, *Basics of Biblical Greek* (Grand Rapids: Zondervan, 2003), §3.1–§3.6; Stanley E. Porter, Jeffrey T. Reed, and Matthew Brook O'Donnell, *Fundamentals of New Testament Greek* (Grand Rapids: Eerdmans, 2010), §1.3; Benjamin L. Merkle and Robert L. Plummer, *Beginning with New Testament Greek: An Introductory Study of the Grammar and Syntax of the New Testament* (Nashville: B&H Academic, 2020), §1.4. It should be noted, however, that Mounce avoids some of the problems above by positing German ü for υ and alternative pronunciations of ζ.

The pronunciation of ευ and ηυ as [ju] implies either that /ju/ is a phonemic diphthong or that [j] is an allophone of /ε/ and /e/ before the vowel /u/. If the latter is true, then words like θεοῦ = /θεu/ should be pronounced as [θju]. It would also imply that somehow /ε/ and /e/ have an allophone of [j] before ου, but /i/ does not.

The pronunciation of υι as [wi] implies either that /wi/ is a phonemic diphthong or that [w] occurs in the language *only* as an allophone of /u/ before /i/.

The pronunciation of ζ as [dz][10] *could* imply that the [z] sound—whether a /z/ phoneme or a voiced [z] allophone of /s/—exists in the language only immediately after /d/.

It is unlikely that a *real* language would have ever developed such a phonology. Now there are certain forms of "Erasmian," such as the more traditional international version, that are quite tame—ευ is /eu/ and the vowels η and ω are /e/ and /o/—and would not pose such problems for fluent reading. The system above, however, which is taught in many American seminaries, might be more aptly deemed a set of conventions for remembering spelling than a pronunciation system reflecting a coherent phonology.

5.5 Papyri, Inscriptions, Manuscripts, and Textual Criticism

As someone who has worked extensively in the fields of papyrology, epigraphy, manuscript studies, and textual criticism, I have found reading this ancient material with a historical Koine Greek pronunciation entirely unremarkable. What I mean is that I rarely feel out of place or out of my element with my pronunciation. Sometimes variant spellings even go unnoticed because they do not present any difficulty or incongruence with the historical pronunciation I have come to use. Because "Erasmian" pronunciation is ultimately shaped around standard spelling

---

10. Note that this fourth example is partly a problem because the pronunciation systems outlined in these textbooks do not prescribe a voiced allophone [z] of σ before voiced consonants.

practices, those using an "Erasmian" pronunciation will encounter more difficulty when attempting to read the primary sources in their primary settings. A quick glance at the thousands of spelling interchanges in the Judeo-Palestinian papyri and epigraphy cited in the larger volume is all that is necessary to underscore this point.

As far as textual criticism goes, Paul Karageorgis has collected scores of examples of cases where a historical Koine Greek pronunciation helps explain some of the textual variants in the early New Testament witnesses, many of which are relevant for interpretation and exegesis. For example, the variant readings of εἰ δὲ 'but if [you call yourself a Jew]' and ἴδε 'look, [you are called a Jew]' in Romans 2:17 are easily explained in light of the merger of ει and ι and the similar pronunciations [iˌðɛ] and ['iðɛ], respectively. The variants ἔχομεν 'we have [peace with God]' and ἔχωμεν 'let us have/we should have [peace with God]' in Romans 5:1 are similarly explained in light of the merger of ω and ο and the identical pronunciation ['ɛxomen]. Finally, the variants ἑταίροις 'companions' and ἑτέροις 'others' in Matthew 11:16 might be explained in light of the merger of αι and ε and the identical pronunciation [ɛ'tɛrys].[11]

Pronunciation is certainly not the only relevant factor in such cases, but using a historical Koine Greek pronunciation will make the reader (or listener) immediately able to appreciate how such variant readings might have arisen. In fact, early Christians may have debated about the proper interpretation of ['ɛxomen] in Romans 5:1 (with respect to its potential modal meaning) even if they were not dealing with a manuscript that had an ω. After all, spelling was neither standardized nor depended upon in the way that it is today. Moreover, most early Christians who "accessed" the text would have done so by hearing it rather than by seeing the original spelling of the manuscript.

11. Paul Karageorgis, "An Examination of the Development of the Pronunciation of Greek and How It Affected the Textual Transmission of the New Testament and Its Consequences on Meaning and Doctrine," (2016): https://www.academia.edu/3767024/An_Examination_of_the_Development_of_the_Pronunciation_of_Greek_and_How_it_Affected_the_Textual_Transmission_of_the_New_Testament_and_its_Consequences_on_Meaning_and_Doctrine, 14–22.

5.6 OPEN THE DOORS TO ELLAÐA

The so-called "revival" of the Hebrew language and the subsequent establishment of the state of Israel was a watershed for Biblical Hebrew studies. It "suddenly" meant that there were now millions of native Hebrew speakers using a form of Hebrew comparable (but by no means identical) to that of the Hebrew Bible. Israeli scholars and universities soon came to be world-renowned in Biblical Hebrew studies. Naturally, authentic and fluent Hebrew language material became available in scores of different contexts and media (newspaper, radio, television, film, YouTube, etc.). Eventually, many nonnative learners and teachers of Biblical Hebrew outside of Israel realized just how helpful learning Modern Hebrew would be for gaining reading proficiency in Biblical Hebrew. For many decades now, aspiring scholars of Biblical Hebrew have been making use of the invaluable resource that is Modern Hebrew with its language community of millions of native speakers to help them in their study of the ancient language.

It is a bit of a wonder, then, why the same sort of attention has not been afforded to Greece and (Modern) Greek. After all, unlike Hebrew, there has never been a moment in the last several thousand years where Greek lacked a sizeable L1 (i.e., mother-tongue language) community. Koine Greek has been and is regularly recited in Greek Orthodox churches as part of the liturgy to this day. Plenty of Greek scholars regularly publish linguistic work on Classical and Koine Greek (and always have) in Modern Greek. Although it is probably true that Modern Hebrew is a bit closer to Biblical Hebrew (morphologically) than Modern Greek is to Koine, these differences should not (and do not) prevent Modern Greek from serving a similar role for students of New Testament Greek as Modern Hebrew does for students of Biblical Hebrew.

Anyone using a historical Koine pronunciation system or a Neohellenic (Modern Greek) pronunciation system will have this invaluable resource wide open to them from the very beginning of their Greek study. They can come home from "Introduction to New Testament Greek" and listen to φεγγαράκι μου λαμπρό 'My Little Bright Moon'—the Greek version of "Twinkle, Twinkle, Little Star"—and already recognize phrases like στον ουρανό 'in the sky' (cf. Matt. 14:19 εἰς τὸν οὐρανόν) and τοῦ θεοῦ τὰ πράγματα 'the things/works of God' (cf. Origen, *Expositio in Proverbia*, 17.200.49: τὰ πράγματα τοῦ θεου). It may also help them feel more connected with the culture and people of Greece. Their study of Koine or New Testament Greek will offer them a head start, rather than a hindrance, in learning to speak with Greeks. This cannot be said about those using the "Erasmian" pronunciation. All in all, using a historical (or Neohellenic) pronunciation of Koine Greek will open one up to countless linguistic and cultural resources that will prove invaluable for growing in one's understanding of New Testament Greek and Greek in general.

5.7 Conclusions: Pronunciation Does Matter

Does pronunciation really matter? The fact that this is a question that even requires a chapter-length defense demonstrates how different Koine Greek is treated from other languages that we learn and teach. Most students and scholars would be embarrassed to walk into a French, German, or Arabic language classroom and ask, "Does pronunciation really matter?" The question would be almost nonsensical. If Koine Greek is every bit as real a language as French, German, or Arabic, then its chronological remoteness does not change its nature with respect to the relevance of pronunciation. Anyone seriously attempting to gain advanced proficiency in a language must give careful attention to pronunciation at some point. In the particular case of Koine Greek and the present state of the field, I have shown that a historical Koine pronunciation will (i) help learners experience and process the language the way the ancients did, (ii) aid in vocabulary acquisition, (iii) promote fluent reading by avoiding incoherent phonological systems that are unlikely to reflect real language, (iv) facilitate the reading of primary sources (papyri, inscriptions, manuscripts) and text-critical work, and (v) open the doors to the many linguistic and cultural resources of Modern Greek (and Greece). Surely, all of that matters.

Appendix: Practice Reading (Transcribed Texts)

I n the following practice texts, the first line contains the Greek text of the New Testament, the second line contains the phonemic representation of this text in IPA transcription, and the third line contains the phonetic representation of this text in IPA transcription. It is thus the third line that reflects the actual pronunciation of the Greek text. Recordings of these texts in the pronunciation recommended in this volume can be found at KoineGreek.com/audio.

MATTHEW 6:9B–13 (BASED ON CODEX VATICANUS)

πάτερ	ἡμῶν	ὁ	ἐν	τοῖς	οὐρανοῖς		
páter	emón	o	εn	týs	uranýs		
'pater	e'mọn	ọ	ε(n)	'dys̱	ura'nys̱		

ἁγιασθήτω	τὸ	ὄνομά	σου				
ayiasθéto	to	ónomá	su				
aja'sθetọ	tọ	'ọnọ'ma	s̱u				

ἐλθέτω	ἡ	βασιλεία	σου	γενηθήτω	τὸ	θέλημά	σου
elθéto	e	βasilía	su	γeneθéto	to	θélemá	su
el'θetọ	e	βas̱i'lia	s̱u	jene'θetọ	tọ	'θele'ma	s̱u

ὡς	ἐν	οὐρανῷ	καὶ	ἐπὶ	γῆς		
os	εn	uranó	kε	εpí	γés		
ọs̱	εn	ura'nọ	cε	ε'pi	'jes̱		

τὸν	ἄρτον	ἡμῶν	τὸν	ἐπιούσιον	δὸς	ἡμῖν	σήμερον
ton	árton	emón	ton	epiúsion	δós	emín	sémeron
tọn	'artọn	e'mọ(n)	dọn	ε'pçus̱çọn	'δọs̱	e'min	'semerọn

καὶ	ἄφες	ἡμῖν	τὰ	ὀφειλήματα	ἡμῶν		
kε	áφes	emín	ta	οφilémata	emón		
cε	'aφes̱	e'mi(n)	da	ọφi'lemata	e'mọn		

ὡς	καὶ	ἡμεῖς	ἀφήκαμεν	τοῖς	ὀφειλέταις	ἡμῶν	
os	kε	emís	aφékamen	týs	oφilétes	emón	
ọs̱	cε	e'mis̱	a'φekamε(n)	'dys̱	ọφi'letes̱	e'mọn	

καὶ	μὴ	εἰσενέγκῃς	ἡμᾶς	εἰς	πειρασμόν		
kε	mé	isenénkes	emás	is	pirasmón		
cε	'me	is̱e'nε(ɲ)jes̱	e'mas̱	is̱	pira'zmọn		

ἀλλὰ	ῥῦσαι	ἡμᾶς	ἀπὸ	τοῦ	πονηροῦ		
alá	rýsε	emás	apó	tú	ponerú		
a'la	'rys̱ε	e'mas̱	a'pọ	'tu	pọne'ru		

LUKE 15:4–6 (BASED ON CODEX VATICANUS)

τίς	ἄνθρωπος	ἐξ	ὑμῶν	ἔχων	ἑκατὸν	πρόβατα
tís	ánthropos	eks	ymón	éxon	ekatón	próbata
'tiʂ	'anθρορος	ekʂ	y'mon	'exon	eka'tọ(n)	'brọβata
καὶ	ἀπολέσας	ἐξ	αὐτῶν	ἓν		
kε	apolésas	eks	aφtón	én		
cε	apọ'lesaʂ	ekʂ	a'φtọn	'εn		
οὐ	καταλείπει	τὰ	ἐνενήκοντα	ἐννέα	ἐν	τῇ	ἐρήμῳ
u	katalípi	ta	εnεnékonta	εnéa	εn	té	εrémo
u	kata'lipi	ta	εnε'nekọ(n)da	ε'nεa	ε(n)	'de	ε'remọ
καὶ	πορεύεται	ἐπὶ	τὸ	ἀπολωλὸς	ἕως	εὕρῃ	αὐτό
kε	poréβetε	εpí	to	apololós	éos	εύρῃ	aφtó
cε	pọ'reβetε	ε'pi	tọ	apọlọ'lọʂ	'εọʂ	'εβre	a'φtọ
καὶ	εὑρὼν	ἐπιτίθησιν	ἐπὶ	τοὺς	ὤμους	αὐτοῦ	χαίρων
kε	εβrón	εpitíθεsin	εpí	tus	ómus	aφtú	xéron
cε	ε'βρọn	εpi'tiθεʂin	ε'pi	tuʂ	'ọmuʂ	a'φtu	'çερọn
καὶ	ἐλθὼν	εἰς	τὸν	οἶκον			
kε	εlθón	is	ton	ýkon			
cε	εl'θọn	iʂ	tọn	'ykọn			
συγκαλεῖ	τοὺς	φίλους	καὶ	τοὺς	γείτονας	λέγων	αὐτοῖς
synkalí	tus	φílus	kε	tus	yítonas	léɣon	aφtýs
sy(ŋ)ga'li	tuʂ	'φiluʂ	cε	tuz	'jitọnaʐ	'lεɣọn	a'φtyʂ
συγχάρητέ	μοι						
synxáreté	my						
syŋ'xɑre'tε	my						
ὅτι	εὗρον	τὸ	πρόβατόν	μου	τὸ	ἀπολωλός	
óti	éβron	to	próβatón	mu	to	apololós	
'ọti	'εβρọ(n)	dọ	'prọβa'tọn	mu	tọ	apọlọ'lọʂ	

JOHN 1:1–5 (BASED ON CODEX VATICANUS)

ἐν	ἀρχῇ	ἦν	ὁ	λόγος
εn	arxé	én	o	lóγos
εn	ar'çe	'en	o̧	'lo̧γo̧s

καὶ	ὁ	λόγος	ἦν	πρὸς	τὸν	θεόν
kε	o	lóγos	én	prós	ton	θεón
cε	o̧	'lo̧γo̧s	'e(n)	'bro̧s	to̧n	θε'o̧n

καὶ	θεὸς	ἦν	ὁ	λόγος
kε	θεós	én	o	lóγos
cε	θε'o̧s	'en	o̧	'lo̧γo̧s

οὗτος	ἦν	ἐν	ἀρχῇ	πρὸς	τὸν	θεόν
útos	én	εn	arxé	prós	ton	θεón
'uto̧s	'en	εn	ar'çe	'pro̧s	to̧n	θε'o̧n

πάντα	δι'	αὐτοῦ	ἐγένετο
pánta	ði	aφtú	εγéneto
'pa(n)da	ði	a'φtu	ε'jeneto̧

καὶ	χωρὶς	αὐτοῦ	ἐγένετο	οὐδὲ	ἓν	ὃ	γέγονεν
kε	xorís	aφtú	εγéneto	uðé	én	ó	γéγonεn
cε	xo̧'ris	a'φtu	ε'jeneto̧	u'ðe	'εn	'o̧	'jeγo̧nεn

ἐν	αὐτῷ	ζωὴ	ἦν
εn	aφtó	zoé	én
εn	a'φto̧	zo̧'e	'en

καὶ	ἡ	ζωὴ	ἦν	τὸ	φῶς	τῶν	ἀνθρώπων
kε	e	zoé	én	to	φós	tón	anθrópon
cε	e	zo̧'e	'e(n)	do̧	'φo̧s	'to̧n	an'θro̧po̧n

καὶ	τὸ	φῶς	ἐν	τῇ	σκοτίᾳ	φαίνει
kε	to	φós	εn	té	skotía	φéni
cε	to̧	'φo̧s	ε(n)	'de	sko̧'tia	'φeni

καὶ	ἡ	σκοτία	αὐτὸ	οὐ	κατέλαβεν
kε	e	skotía	aφtó	u	katélaβen
cε	e	sko̧'tia	a'φto̧	u	ka'tεlaβen

Selected Bibliography

For a complete bibliography, see the larger volume. What appears below is a topical bibliography of the works cited in this short volume.

Historical Greek Phonology

Al-Jallad, Ahmad. "Graeco-Arabica I: The Southern Levant." In *Arabic in Context*, edited by Ahmad Al-Jallad, 99–186. Leiden: Brill, 2017.

Allen, James P. *Ancient Egyptian Phonology*. Cambridge: Cambridge University Press, 2020.

Allen, W. Sidney. *Vox Graeca: A Guide to the Pronunciation of Classical Greek*. Cambridge: Cambridge University Press, 1968.

Arnold, Edward V., and Robert S. Conway. *The Restored Pronunciation of Greek and Latin*. Cambridge: Cambridge University Press, 1895.

Berenguer-Sánchez, José Antonio, and Juan Rodríguez Somolinos. "Sur la flexion nominale en -ις, -ιν." In *Papyrologica Vindobonensia. Akten des 23. Internationalen Papyrologenkongresses. 1*, 39–48. Vienna: Verlag der Österreichischen Akademie der Wissenschaften, 2007.

Blackie, John Stuart. *The Pronunciation of Greek; Accent and Quantity: A Philological Inquiry*. Edinburgh/London: Sutherland and Knox/Simpkin, Marshall & Co., 1852.

Blass, F., A. Debrunner, and Robert W. Funk. *A Greek Grammar of the New Testament and Other Early Christian Literature*. Cambridge/Chicago: Cambridge University Press/University of Chicago Press, 1961.

Brixhe, Claude. "Le changement <ΙΟ> → <Ι> en pamphylien, en laconien et dans la koiné d'Egypte." *Verbum* 16 (1994): 219–41.

Bubenik, Vit. *Hellenistic and Roman Greece as a Sociolinguistic Area*. Amsterdam/
Philadelphia: John Benjamins, 1989.

Clackson, James. "A Greek Papyrus in Armenian Script." *Zeitschrift für Papyrologie und Epigraphik* 129 (2000): 223–58.

D'Angour, Armand. "Musica Linguae, Lingua Musicae." Presentation at Classics in Praxis at Delphi Economic Forum VII, Delphi, Greece, April 8, 2022. https://www.armand-dangour.com/2022/04/musica-linguae-lingua-musicae/.

Depauw, Mark, and Joanne Stolk. "Linguistic Variation in Greek Papyri: Towards a New Tool for Quantitative Study." *Greek, Roman, and Byzantine Studies* 55 (2015): 196–220.

Devine, Andrew M., and Lawrence D. Stephens. *The Prosody of Greek Speech*. Oxford: Oxford University Press, 1994.

Feyerabend, Karl. *Handy Dictionary of the Greek and English Languages*. New York: David McKay Company, 1918.

Geldart, Edmund M. *The Modern Greek Language in Its Relation to Ancient Greek*. Oxford: Clarendon, 1870.

Goldstein, David. "Pitch." In *Encyclopedia of Ancient Greek Language and Linguistics*, edited by Georgios K. Giannakis, Vit Bubenik, Emilio Crespo, Chris Golston, Alexandra Lianeri, Silvia Luraghi, and Stephanos Matthaios, 100–101. Leiden: Brill, 2014.

Golston, Chris. "Stress." In *Encyclopedia of Ancient Greek Language and Linguistics*, edited by Georgios K. Giannakis, Vit Bubenik, Emilio Crespo, Chris Golston, Alexandra Lianeri, Silvia Luraghi, and Stephanos Matthaios, Leiden/Boston: Brill, 2014.

Holton, David, Peter Mackridge, and Irene Philippaki-Warburton. *Greek: A Comprehensive Grammar*. New York: Routledge, 2012.

Horrocks, Geoffrey. *Greek: A History of the Language and Its Speakers*. Oxford: Wiley-Blackwell, 2014.

Kantor, Benjamin. "The Thirteenth-Century Hebrew Tradition of the Jews of Southern Italy: Greek Transcriptions of Hebrew Words in Nikolaos of Otranto's 'Disputation against the Jews'." *Leshonenu* 82, no. 3 (2020): 148–84 [Hebrew].

———. "The LXX and Historical Greek Phonology: Orthography, Phonology, and Transcriptions." *Journal for the Study of Judaism* 53 (2022): 1–33. https://doi.org/10.1163/15700631-bja10060.

Keil, Heinrich. *Velius Longus: De Orthographia*. Leipzig: Teubner, 1880.

Petrounias, E. B. "The Pronunciation of Classical Greek." In *A History of Ancient Greek: From the Beginnings to Late Antiquity*, edited by A.-F. Christidis, 556–70. Cambridge: Cambridge University Press, 2007.

Solomon, Jon. "The Seikilos Inscription: A Theoretical Analysis." *American Journal of Philology* 107, no. 4 (1986): 455–79.

Sturtevant, Edgar H. *The Pronunciation of Greek and Latin*. Chicago: Ares, 1940.

Wright, Wilmer Cave. *Philostratus, the Lives of the Sophists; Eunapius, Lives of the Philosophers*. Loeb Classical Library 134. Cambridge: Harvard University Press, 2015.

KOINE GREEK DIALECTOLOGY

Brixhe, Claude. *Essai sur le grec anatolien au début de notre ère.* Nancy: Presses Universitaires de Nancy, 1987.

———. "Linguistic Diversity in Asia Minor during the Empire: *Koine* and Non-Greek Languages." In *A Companion to the Ancient Greek Language*, edited by Egbert J. Bakker, 228–52. Malden: Wiley-Blackwell, 2010.

Gignac, Francis Thomas. *Phonology.* Vol. 1 of *A Grammar of the Greek Papyri of the Roman and Byzantine Periods.* Milan: Istituto Editoriale Cisalpino, 1976.

Leon, Harry Joshua. "The Language of the Greek Inscriptions from the Jewish Catacombs of Rome." *Transactions and Proceedings of the American Philological Association* 58 (1927): 210–33.

Mayser, Edwin, and Hans Schmoll. *Grammatik der griechischen Papyri aus der Ptolemäerzeit: Band 1: Laut- und Wortlehre.* Berlin: de Gruyter, 1970.

Nachmanson, Ernst. *Laute und Formen der magnetischen Inschriften.* Uppsala: Almqvist & Wiksells, 1904.

Rüsch, Edmund. *Grammatik der delphischen Inschriften. I. Lautlehre.* Berlin: Weidmannsche Buchhandlung, 1914.

Schweizer, Eduard. *Grammatik der pergamenischen Inschriften: Beiträge zur Laut- und Flexionslehre der gemeingriechischen Sprache.* Berlin: Weidmannsche Buchhandlung, 1898.

———. *Griechische Grammatik: Erster Band: Allgemeiner Teil. Lautlehre. Wortbildung. Flexion.* München: Beck, 1939.

Slavova, Mirena. *Phonology of the Greek Inscriptions in Bulgaria.* Stuttgart: Franz Steiner Verlag, 2004.

Teodorsson, Sven-Tage. *The Phonology of Ptolemaic Koine.* Göteborg: Acta Universitatis Gothoburgensis, 1977.

———. *The Phonology of Attic in the Hellenistic Period.* Göteborg: Acta Universitatis Gothoburgensis, 1978.

Threatte, Leslie. *The Grammar of Attic Inscriptions I: Phonology.* Berlin: de Gruyter, 1980.

PHONOLOGY, PHONETICS, AND HISTORICAL LINGUISTICS

Campbell, Lyle. *Historical Linguistics: An Introduction.* Cambridge: MIT Press, 1999.

Hyman, Larry. "Universals in Phonology." *Linguistic Review* 25, no. 1–2 (2008): 345–90.

Janda, Richard D., and Brian D. Joseph. "Reconsidering the Canons of Sound-Change: Towards a 'Big Bang' Theory." In *Historical Linguistics 2001: Selected Papers from the 15th International Conference on Historical Linguistics, Melbourne, 13–17 August 2001*, edited by Barry J. Blake and Kate Burridge, 205–20. Amsterdam/Philadelphia: John Benjamins, 2003.

Ladefoged, Peter. *A Course in Phonetics*. Fort Worth: Harcourt College Publishers, 2001.

Martin, Andrew, and Sharon Peperkamp. "Speech Perception and Phonology." Page 2334–56. In *Phonological Interfaces*, edited by Marc van Oostendrop, Colin J. Ewen, Elizabeth Hume, and Keren Rice. Vol. 4 of *The Blackwell Companion to Phonology*. Malden: Wiley-Blackwell, 2011.

Miller, Brett, Neil Myler, and Bert Vaux. "Phonology in Universal Grammar." In *The Oxford Handbook of Universal Grammar*, edited by Ian Roberts, 153–82. Oxford: Oxford University Press, 2016.

Greek Pronunciation in the Academy

Ballabriga, Alain. "Philhellénisme et prononciation du grec. À propos de la 'Dissertation sur la prononciation grecque' de Fleury de Lécluse." *Anabases* 3 (2006): 57–77.

Barnard, Jody A. "The 'Erasmian' Pronunciation of Greek: Whose Error Is It?" *Erasmus Studies* 37 (2017): 109–32.

Buth, Randall. "Ἡ Κοινὴ Προφορά *Koiné Pronunciation:* Notes on the Pronunciation System of Koiné Greek." Biblical Language Center (2012): 1–10.

Bywater, Ingram. *The Erasmian Pronunciation of Greek and Its Precursors: Jerome Aleander, Aldus Manutius, Antonio of Lebrixa: A Lecture*. Oxford: Oxford University Press, 1908.

Campbell, Constantine. *Advances in the Study of Greek: New Insights for Reading the New Testament*. Grand Rapids: Zondervan, 2015.

Caragounis, Chrys C. "The Error of Erasmus and Un-Greek Pronunciations of Greek." *Filología Neotestamentaria* 8 (1995): 151–85.

Cohen, Gary G., and C. Norman Sellers. "The Case for Modern Pronunciation of Biblical Languages." *Grace Theological Journal* 5 (1984): 197–203.

Dickey, Eleanor. *Colloquia Monacensia–Einsidlensia, Leidense–Stephani, and Stephani*. Vol. 1 of *The Colloquia of the Hermeneumata Pseudodositheana*. Cambridge: Cambridge University Press, 2012.

———. *Colloquium Harleianum, Colloquium Montepessulanum, Colloquium Celtis, and Fragments*. Vol. 2 of *The Colloquia of the Hermeneumata Pseudodositheana*. Cambridge: Cambridge University Press, 2015.

Dillon, Matthew. "The Erasmian Pronunciation of Ancient Greek: A New Perspective." *Classical World* 94, no. 4 (2001): 323–34.

Drerup, Engelbert. *Die Schulaussprache des Griechischen von der Renaissance bis zur Gegenwart, im Rahmen einer allgemeinen Geschichte des griechischen Unterrichts. Erster Teil: Von XV bis zum Ende des XVII Jahrhunderts*. Paderborn: Schöningh, 1930.

GreekPod101.com. "Greek Pronunciation - Vowels." (2015): Accessed 26 October, 2021. https://youtu.be/Xql6qZ3lpUo.

Karageorgis, Paul. "An Examination of the Development of the Pronunciation of Greek and How It Affected the Textual Transmission of the New Testament and Its Consequences on Meaning and Doctrine." (2016): https://www.ac ademia.edu/37670241/An_Examination_of_the_Development_of_the_Pro nunciation_of_Greek_and_How_it_Affected_the_Textual_Transmission_of _the_New_Testament_and_its_Consequences_on_Meaning_and_Doctrine.

McDiarmid, John F. "Recovering Republican Eloquence: John Cheke versus Stephen Gardiner on the Pronunciation of Greek." *History of European Ideas* 38, no. 3 (2012): 338–51.

McNeal, Richard A. "Hellenist and Erasmian." *Glotta* 53, no. 1/2 (1975): 81–101.

Merkle, Benjamin L., and Robert L. Plummer. *Beginning with New Testament Greek: An Introductory Study of the Grammar and Syntax of the New Testament*. Nashville: B&H Academic, 2020.

Morwood, James. *The Oxford Grammar of Classical Greek*. New York: Oxford University Press, 2001.

———. *The Teaching of Classics*. Cambridge: Cambridge University Press, 2003.

Mounce, William D. *Basics of Biblical Greek*. Grand Rapids: Zondervan, 2003.

Päll, Janika. "Far Away from Byzantium: Pronunciation and Orthography of Greek in the 17th Century Estonia." In *Byzantino-Nordica 2004: Papers Presented at the International Symposium of Byzantine Studies Held on 7-11 May 2004 in Tartu, Estonia*, edited by Ivo Volt and Janika Päll, 86–119. Tartu: Tartu University Press, 2005.

Petrounias, E. B. "The Pronunciation of Ancient Greek in Modern Times." In *A History of Ancient Greek: From the Beginnings to Late Antiquity*, edited by A.-F. Christidis, 1266–79. Cambridge: Cambridge University Press, 2007.

Porter, Stanley E. "So What Have We Learned in the Last Thirty Years of Greek Linguistic Study?" In *Getting into the Text: New Testament Essays in Honor of David Alan Black*, edited by Daniel L. Akin and Thomas W. Hudgins, 9–38. Eugene, OR: Pickwick, 2017.

Porter, Stanley E., Jeffrey T. Reed, and Matthew Brook O'Donnell. *Fundamentals of New Testament Greek*. Grand Rapids: Eerdmans, 2010.

Ranieri, Luke. "Ancient Greek Pronunciation Guide and Discourse on the Inherent Challenges of Establishing a Single Ancient Greek Pronunciation System with Detailed Explanation of the Lucian Pronunciation of Ancient Greek." Published online at LukeRanieri.com, 2021.

Russell, Eugenia. "Book Review Essay: Greek in the Renaissance: Scholarship, Dissemination and Transition." *Renaissance Studies* 25, no. 4 (2011): 585–89.

Theophilus, Michael P. "On the Pronunciation and Interpretation of 'Biblical Greek': A Re-Assessment in Light of the Papyri." Paper presented at the University of Cambridge New Testament Seminar, 6 November 2012.

Zachariou, Philemon. *Reading and Pronouncing Biblical Greek: Historical Pronunciation versus Erasmian.* Eugene, OR: Wipf & Stock, 2020.

PRONUNCIATION IN SECOND LANGUAGE ACQUISITION

Channell, Joanna M. "Vocabulary Acquisition and the Mental Lexicon." In *Meaning and Lexicography*, edited by Jerzy Tomaszczyk and Barbara Lewandowska-Tomaszczyk, 21–30. Philadelphia: John Benjamins, 1990.

Fay, David, and Anne Cutler. "Malapropisms and the Structure of the Mental Lexicon." *Linguistic Inquiry* 8, no. 3 (1977): 505–20.

Murphy, John. "Attending to Word-Stress While Learning New Vocabulary." *English for Specific Purposes* 23, no. 1 (2004): 67–83.

Zhang, Xian, and Xiaofei Lu. "The Relationship between Vocabulary Learning Strategies and Breadth and Depth of Vocabulary Knowledge." *Modern Language Journal* 99, no. 4 (2015): 740–53.